MW01290948

YOUR NEXT CHAPTER

How to Turn the Page and
Create the Life of Your Dreams

ISBN-13: 978-1500938260
ISBN-10: 1500938262

MANNY SCOTT | ORIGINAL FREEDOM WRITER

Design by Signify
Library of Congress Cataloging-in-Publication Data

Scott, Manny
    YOUR NEXT CHAPTER – 1st ed.

ISBN-13: 978-1500938260
ISBN-10: 1500938262

Dedication:

I dedicate this book to all the people in the world who have supported me through the years. You have sent me emails, messages on social media, and letters to thank me for my work, and to encourage me to keep doing it. You know who you are. Thank you!

TABLE OF CONTENTS

TABLE OF CONTENTS

I have invested the last fifteen years of my life trying to give people hope. Often, with a heaviness of heart, I have walked into the darkest places and stood alongside discouraged, depressed, hurting, and hopeless people. As I write this, many of their faces are being breathed upon my remembrance. I see, like it was yesterday, the face of a young man who stopped me in the hallway after I spoke at his school. He was trembling, with a pain in his eyes that was so overwhelming that he could not speak. After I sat with him for a while, he was eventually able to share with me that he had just walked into his front door and found his father dangling from a rope. His dad had committed suicide.

I also see the face of a young, sobbing girl who pulled up her shirt to show me the bruises on her body, and who, through her shaky, desperate cries, said, "I'm bleeding from my private parts. The men are hurting me. They're hurting me. Please help me. Please help me!"

I also see the face of a hardened young man who was reduced to tears as he tried to tell me about his 3-month-old baby sister whose insides were destroyed by his pedophile stepfather.

Then there's the face of the young man who walked up to me, perspiring, with his head hanging, and tears falling from his face. As I hugged him, blood just started gushing from his nose onto my clothes and shoes and onto the gymnasium floor. Through the blood, all he kept saying to me, over and over again, was, "thank you, thank you, thank you, thank you ..."

I have tens of thousands of stories like that weighing heavy on my heart as I write these words. In each case, I have done my best to let every one of those beautiful, bruised people know that I care, that they are loved, and that their lives can get better. I have tried my best to be salt and light for them.

However, my time with them has almost always been rushed. There was always another person in line waiting to talk with me, there was always another speaking engagement, or another flight, or another pressing priority that demanded my attention. Despite my desire to tell those individuals more, and teach them more about how to turn things around in their lives, I have almost always had to leave them with only a tiny fraction of what I really wanted to tell them.

Consequently, this book is my attempt to give a more complete hope and help to people like that. People, who through the tears and pain, through the frustration and discouragement, want to know how to create a better life for themselves and those they love. I'm convinced that in the right hands, at the right time, this book will open someone's eyes, renew someone's hope, and change someone's life. I hope that someone is you.

Manny Scott
January 2015

By picking up this book, you are beginning something that can truly change the quality of your life forever. This book is for those people who, right now, want more out of life, and don't know how to get it. This book is for those who have a feeling in their hearts that they were made for something greater, for something more meaningful, and significant. This book has been written for those who want more, feel like they were created for more, and are determined to take hold of more—more hope, more happiness, more peace, more purpose, more success, more money, and more love.

I should be an alcoholic, a drug addict, an abuser of women, promiscuous, homeless, violent, locked-up, or dead. However, by a string of rather improbable encounters, and some very important decisions, I am relatively sane, completely sober, free, and still very much alive; and, I have some very important things I really want to share with you that can change your life, forever.

I am speaking from experience. I am speaking from the experience of having applied the things in this book to improve my own life. If you know nothing about me, I want to introduce myself to you by giving you a very abbreviated version of my story, just so you can understand where I am coming from.

I was born into a beautiful, but broken, family. My father has been imprisoned my whole life. My stepfather, who was generally a good man, was an alcoholic, and he was at one point addicted to cocaine. There were many nights when my stepfather got drunk or so high that he physically abused my mother. I'll never forget the night that my stepfather grabbed my mother by the back of her head, and he slammed her face through a glass window; and, as a little boy, I literally had to fight for my mother's life. There were nights when I would hear my mother screaming for help, and all I could do was call the police, and beg them to come and save my mother.

My mother, who came from a very broken family herself, tried to find stability for us—but before I was 16 years old, we had already lived in 26 places—not including the cars, the beaches, the alleys, the hotels, the motels, the homeless shelters, and all the other places we stayed. I have lost count of the number of places we slept before I was 16.

There were nights that we would stop at a homeless shelter because we didn't have anywhere else to go, and I would be lying on the floor, with no pillow, no blanket, and no mattress; I was clutching a piece of stale bread, wondering if there was any hope for us. I remember my mother taking off her jacket, laying it over the top of me and softly saying "baby, everything's going to be okay." As much as I wanted to believe my mother, things were not okay. There were some nights when I would be so hungry that I would jump into dumpsters at restaurants and I would tear open bags, sifting through garbage, just to find something to help me make it through the night.

I was the kid that you saw a block away, who made you nervous, so you crossed the street. I was the kid that your parents didn't let you play with. And I was the kid who took all those issues with me to school. I had so many issues that it was hard for me to pay attention in class. But how could I, as a little boy, care about math and integers when my personal life was full of fractions and frictions? How could I care about helping verbs at school, when words never seemed to help me at home? How could I care about the different food groups the body needs to be healthy, when I barely had enough food at home to survive? How could I focus on schoolwork when defending my mother became a regular part of my homework? And, how could I care about going to school when I wasn't even sure I would have a home to go to at night? I used to sit in class, with holes in my pants, holes in my shoes, and with a deflated sense of self. So from kindergarten all the way through high school, something happened to me that made me dislike school more and more. The loneliness, the embarrassment, the awkwardness, the self-consciousness of being the new kid always haunted me. I got tired of not fitting in, tired of not being accepted, and tired of not being invited to join people's groups. I got tired of not being invited to birthday parties, I got tired of being on the outside. So I stopped going to school.

Instead of going home, and instead of going the school, I spent much more of my time in the streets. It was in the streets that I learned how to survive. It was in the streets that I learned how to steal groceries from supermarkets just so I could have food to help me make it through the night. It was in the streets that I met people who were just as broken as me, just as angry as me, just as socially awkward as me, just as desirous of a place to belong as me.

I was running the streets with some of these guys, and it was then that I started smoking marijuana. It was then that I started drinking alcohol. It was in the streets that I began stealing cars and burglarizing homes. I was heading down a path that would have destroyed me. It was in the streets that I learned to play cat and mouse games with police officers. It was in the streets when I learned how to find secret getaways, and back streets; and, where I learned to identify undercover police officers and unmarked cars. It was in the streets that I learned how to survive.

The first semester of my freshman year in high school I earned a 0.6 grade point average. I earned three Fs, two Ds, and one C. I earned a D in physical education. The second semester of my freshman year, my best friend was murdered brutally. When my best friend Alex was killed, something inside of me died with him, and I went into a very dark depression. It was in that dark place that I became very, very angry. I was suicidal. I had gotten to a place emotionally where I really stopped caring about the feelings of other people. Emotionally, I was dead, spiritually, I was dead—everything about me was numb. And I was in such a dark place, such an angry place, that I began thinking of ways, strategizing, to make other people feel my pain. It is indeed true that hurt people, hurt people.

It was in that place of brokenness, that place of darkness, that place of death, that I just gave up—I gave up on life, I gave up on hope, I gave up on loving people, I gave up on any dreams or aspirations I thought I had. And I began saying things like, "people like me, we ain't supposed to make it!" It was in that valley of despair, that quagmire of misery, that place of other lostness, that I gave up, literally.

It was in that place of brokenness that I was walking by Drake Park in Long Beach, California. I saw a bench, and I just sat down on it. On that bench, my soul was crying out with that poet, Paul Laurence Dunbar, who said:

A crust of bread and a corner to sleep in,
a minute to smile and an hour to weep in;
A peck of joy to a pint of trouble,
and never a laugh, but the moans come double;
And that is life.

My heart was in complete agreement with the existentialist philosopher who said, "life is an endless pain with a painful end." I was absolutely convinced that the last paragraph of my life was being written. On that bench, the last period of my life story was about to be penned. On that bench, I was certain in my soul that my story was over …

But a complete stranger sat down next to me and helped me see that my story did not have to be over. He helped me see that I had the power to turn the page; to begin writing a new chapter in my life. He helped me see that my life could get better.

I went back to school and earned As and Bs; I made the honor roll for the first time in my life; I became a standout athlete; I became the first person in my family to graduate from high school; I graduated from U.C. Berkeley with two degrees; I earned my master's degree; I'm working on my Ph.D.; I am a pilot and owner of my own airplane; I am a successful real-estate investor who owns several properties; I'm happily married to the woman of my dreams; I've become the loving father that I never had; and, I now spend over 200 days traveling the world helping people to turn the page, and begin new chapters in their own lives.

How did I make such a drastic turnaround? How did I go from earning Fs and Ds to As and Bs; from being a high school drop-out to having a master's degree, and a Ph.D. in the near future; from being an English as a Second Language (ESL) student to one who can read Greek and Hebrew. How did I go from being "un-teachable" to unstoppable? How did I go from being homeless to having a beautiful home that I love? How did I go from merely fantasizing about flying airplanes to becoming a pilot with my own plane? How did I become a faithful husband even though I had never really seen one growing up? How have I become loving father of three beautiful children even though I have never really seen, close-up, what a good father looks like?

More importantly, how can you go from living beneath your potential to realizing your dreams; from being an "F" student to an "A" student; from being broke to being financially free; from mediocrity to excellence; from living check-to-check to enjoying financial freedom? From here to there, from where you are to where you want to be? How? How? How?

My best answers to those questions are in this book. This book is my understanding about success up to this point in my life. In it, I share the fundamentals that have allowed me to overcome my own obstacles, and make it to this place in my life. If you apply these things to your own life, I have no doubt that your life will get better.

My friend, no matter where you are from, you can create a future that is so much better than your past. Your past does not have to be a prologue to your future. You can achieve tremendous success in the face of incredible challenges, starting today. Right now.

I am absolutely committed in this book to making sure that you are crystal clear about how to turn the page, and begin writing a new chapter in your life. I am committed to helping you achieve your dreams. All that's required of you is two things. Number one, the desire on your part to learn, and number two, your commitment to read this book, and do the assignments that I give you to think about, and work through, as simple or as challenging as the activities may seem at the moment. If you will do that, the things that you used to call dreams will become a part of your daily reality.

As you begin this journey of beginning this next chapter of your life, I want to tell you that I have incredible respect for you, and that I care about you. Even though I may not know you personally, I hope that my caring will come through in the words on these pages. The reason I respect you is because I feel that you and I have kindred spirits. You opened this book, you made an investment, and you are now being proactive about improving the quality of your life. You are ten times further along than ninety percent of the people that you and I will meet on the street or in school. Most people who want to improve the quality of their lives have no clue about what it is they want out of life, and worse, they are not willing to do anything to change it. You're at least searching, and for you to be reading this book says to me that you're willing to do what it takes to be successful, to turn the page, to write new, more fulfilling chapters in your life.

ASSIGNMENT #1
WHAT'S YOUR STORY?

I cannot let this opportunity pass without asking you to do something really important. You just read part of my story. Now I want you to write down yours. What is your story? If you had the opportunity to stand before an audience of strangers in order to tell your story, what would you say? If you have never written your story before, now is the time for you to do so. This book is about you writing "Your Next Chapter." Logically, how can you begin a new chapter if you are not clear about your old chapters? While this book is dedicated to helping you move forward, the truth is that we cannot go forward without you first going backward.

Long before I ever told my story publicly, I was writing, and re-writing, my story privately. It took me a while to craft my story in a way that felt right in my soul. That process helped me learn much more about how the experiences of my past shaped me, good and bad. It also helped me get clear about how I wanted my story to end.

Writing your story can have the same effect on you. So write your story. Be honest with yourself. No one else has to read it; it's for your eyes only. Where were you born? Write about your parents and ancestors and how they shaped your upbringing. Write about your life growing up. Write about your neighborhood, and how it shaped you. Also, write about your experiences in school, good and bad. Write about your self-image, your successes, your failures. Write about the experiences that shaped you, good and bad. Were you popular? Wealthy?

Spoiled? Vain? Selfish? Proud? Conceited? Or were you home-less? Hungry? Molested? Abused? Overweight? Socially awk-ward? A loner? … What is your story?

Write until you feel you have gotten your story out. When you are finished, re-read it, over and over again. If you want, you can email me a copy of your story at ync@mannyscott.com. If you are not uncomfortable sharing it with me, then I'd love to read it. In any case, whether you share it with me or not, congratulations on beginning this new chapter of your life!

CHAPTER 2
YOUR POWER

I trust you have written your story. If you have not, then stop reading right now, and go finish that first assignment. I have been helping people a long time, and I have never seen people make it to step number two if they did not first take step number one. Step number one involves you writing your story down, and getting clear about it.

Okay, now, I want you to give yourself an honest assessment of where you are in your life right now. If you had to give yourself a score between 1-10, what would you give yourself in the following areas?

---

1. In terms of your overall development as a person, on a scale between 1-10, what score would you give yourself? Are you where you want to be? Explain.

---

2. Physically, on a scale between 1-10, what score do you give yourself? Why?

3. Educationally/Professionally, are you where you want to be? On a scale of 1-10, what score do you give yourself? Why?

4. Financially, on a scale between 1-10, how well are you making and managing your money? Explain.

5. Materially, on a scale between 1-10, do you have most of the things you need or want?

6. Relationally, on a scale between 1-10, how healthy are your relationships with your family, friends, classmates and co-workers? Explain.

7. Spiritually, on a scale between 1-10, how are you doing?

Your responses to the above questions tell a story about you.

What story emerges about your life? Are you where you want to be, or do you have a ways to go? If you are satisfied with where you are in your life right now, congratulations! You can stop reading, and put down this book. Go and enjoy your life. Keep doing what you've been doing, and you will probably keep getting what you've been getting.

However, if you are not *where* you want to be; if you are not *who* you want to be; and, if you do not *have* what you want to have, then continue reading.

If you are not where you want to be in life, you need to understand the five things that have brought you to this place. You are who you are, and you are where you are because you have been shaped by at least five forces. All of us are shaped by at least five things. First, we are shaped by **human nature**. Like other members of the humanity, we all have a survival instinct. We have a need to survive. We want to feel safe and secure. We want to be successful and significant. We enjoy spontaneity, novelty, and adventure. We like to laugh, have fun, and experience love. We all have the ability to feel emotions such as fear, anger, love, hope, joy, sadness, and so on. We have no ability to change human nature's impact on us.

We are also shaped by **heredity**. All of us inherited certain traits or genes from our parents and ancestors. Our eye color, our skin color, and our body types were passed down to us from someone in our family tree. We can't really change our genes. We can change how we look by getting plastic surgery or putting on makeup or contact lenses, but we cannot change the genes that were passed down to us.

Third, we are also shaped by our **environment** or **culture**. What is culture? Culture is an agricultural word that comes from the Latin verb, *colere*, which means "to tend, guard, cultivate, or till." In most Western languages, culture commonly refers to one's cultivation or refinement through formal education. So, in most Western countries, when we say someone is "cultured," we are usually referring to someone who has an *informed* love for the music, poetry, wine, museums, and literature. This is culture in the most superficial sense of the word.

Culture in the broader sense refers to patterns of thinking, feeling, and potential acting, which you learned throughout your lifetime. For example: when you were born and your parents took you home from the hospital and raised you, they modeled for you how you should talk, walk, eat, greet, dress, sleep, live, love and so on. They taught you about who belonged in your group, and who did not. They taught you how people who are in your group should think, feel, and behave. They taught you how to properly relate to people in your family, in your neighborhood, in your environment.

Before you even aware of it, your brain was programmed with those same patterns of thinking, feeling, and potential behaving. You just took those patterns for granted. Most of us never really question those patterns, because we have had them for so long. Without getting too technical, all I am trying to get you to understand right now is that you have been programmed with cultural values that have shaped what you believe, how you feel, and how you behave.

In addition to being shaped by human nature, heredity, and your culture, you have also been shaped by your **personality**.

Even though you share the same nature as other humans, and you share the same culture with others, your personality sets you apart from others. Your personality, though influenced by human nature, and influenced by your cultural background, is something that is unique to you.

You might be an introvert who feels drained when you're around crowds; or, you might be an extrovert who gets energized when you are around other people. You might have a dominant personality that drives you to get things done. Or you might have an influential personality, which enables you to work well with other people. Or, you might have a more precise personality, which compels you to be very meticulous with minute details. Or, you might have a very supportive personality, which leads you to prefer to work behind the scenes. No matter what your personality is, it is unique to you, and it has a great deal to do with who you are and where you are in life.

Fifth, you have been shaped by your **decisions**. You have been given the ability to choose what to believe, how to feel, and how to behave. Maybe as a child, you did not believe you had as much freedom to make your own decisions, but the fact is, you have been making decisions your whole life. Even when you did not want to obey your parents, you chose (you decided) to do so, probably to avoid being punished. Nonetheless, you still had the freedom to decide whether you were going to do what they said or not. That was your decision.

Who you are, and where you are, right now in your life is the result of your human nature, your heredity, your culture, your personality, and your personal decisions; but, the most powerful one of them all is your decisions. Your power to decide is more powerful than your heredity, cultural back-

ground, and personality combined, because it's your decisions, not your conditions, that determine your deeds and your destiny. It's your decisions, not your skin color; it's your decisions, not your family; it's your decisions, not your neighborhood; it's your decisions that ultimately determine the quality of your future.

Etymologically, the word, "decide," comes from the Latin compound word, *decidere* (de- which means "off"+ caedere, which means "to cut"). To decide, then, literally means "to cut off." To decide means to commit, then cut. It means we have committed ourselves to achieve a certain goal, and we have cut ourselves off from any other possibility. When we make a decision about something, we are committing ourselves to think, feel, or behave a *specific way* by simultaneously cutting ourselves off from thinking, feeling, or behaving any other way.

I heard someone say that if you want to take over an island, you must burn the boats. You must eliminate any possibility that you, or anybody else, will leave the island. You must burn the boats. You must cut yourself off from being able to leave that island.

You have the power to cut things out of your life right now. You have the power to cut some people off right now. You have the power to cut some habits off, right now. You can cut beliefs, feelings, and behaviors off, right now, just by making a decision to do so.

This leads to what the main point of this chapter: Turning the Page! When you make a decision, you are committing to achieve a specific goal, and cutting yourself from any other possibility; and, when you turn the page, you are not merely committing to anything in general, but you are committing yourself to creating a better life, and are cutting yourself off from any other possibility.

When you turn the page, you begin taking responsibility for your life from this day forward. When you turn the page, you give up your expectation or hope that someone else is going to come into your life to fix it. When you turn the page, you take ownership of your life, the good, the bad, and the ugly. You give up your right to blame others, your heredity, or your environment for your problems. Please hear me well: I'm not saying that others are not responsible for some of the pain you feel in your life, because they may very well be culpable and worthy of blame. What I am saying is that your situation will never get better if you wallow in blame and anger. That will get you nowhere.

What I'm saying is *although you cannot control your past, your parents, or your history, you can control how you respond to life from this day forward.* You can dwell on the past, or you can turn the page, and create a better future. You can blame your father or mother for abandoning you, or you can turn the page and become the kind of parent you always wanted. Sure, you can blame others for your problems, or you can turn the page, and work tirelessly to eliminate those problems. That's what it means to turn the page. Is there poverty, and systemic evil, and government corruption? Absolutely! Do we still have a criminal justice system in America that is deeply flawed? Of course we do. Do we have a school system that needs to be reformed? No doubt about it. But what are you going to do about it? Cry, complain, gripe and moan? Or, are we going to turn the page, and begin working toward addressing those problems?

I am where I am in life, not because the world is fair and just; I am here because, despite the wrongs that have tried to cripple and destroy me, I decided to turn the page, and work proactively to improve my life and the life of others.

That's what it means to turn the page. It means that you have committed yourself to achieving a specific goal, and you have cut yourself off from any other possibility. It means eliminating the hope that someone else is going to see your gifts and talents and ask you to use them for their benefit. No! To turn the page means that you are going to take the edge of the page of your own life story, and you are going to turn that page yourself. You are going to proactively advance the quality of your life, one page, and one chapter, one decision at a time.

Think about it. What can you do when the business that you knew was your ticket to financial freedom has failed? When the toy you used to love breaks on you? When the best friend you believed you would grow up with moves away? When the application to your dream school gets rejected? Or when the promotion you were hoping on is given to someone else? Or when the dream of a perfect marriage has died because of some tragic discovery? When the company you loved has now downsized, or restructured you out of a job? Or when the physique that used to be so irresistible has become flabby? What do you do when the influence you once had has now died because of some misunderstanding? What can you do when the dependability of those who raised you is now gone, and it's now your responsibility to support them? Or the capacity to give birth has now left you because of life's swift transitions? What do you do when that which once defined your manhood is no longer attentive? Or when the friends you grew old with have now passed on? What do you do when the vehicle, the thing, the strategy, the action plan, or the person you hoped would take you to your destination has failed you?

What else can you do, but turn the page? There's no reason to try erasing your mistake, to backspace it, to white it out. That chapter of your life has already been completed, the ink has already dried, and the manuscript has already been sent to publication. All you can do is turn the page. No need in trying to re-write the chapter, burn the book, or throw it away. It is done. You have to learn from it and turn the page.

Maybe before you picked up this book, you thought your "book" was finished, but the fact is, there is another chapter for your life. If you're still alive, then there is still hope. If you are still breathing, then there is still time for you to begin a new chapter. It can be greater than the last one. But you have to turn the page.

Maybe you have been re-reading that last chapter, or have been internalizing the fact that you didn't get that job, or you didn't get that promotion; or you didn't get that guy or girl; or you didn't get that home; or you didn't get into that school; or, you didn't do well in that subject. Or, or, or ... Stop! You can't change it! It's done! You have to turn the page!

No matter where you are from, you have the power to turn the page. You have the power to make decisions that will change the quality of your life forever. Right now, you have that power. It is something your creator gave to you at birth. It is a power that you have at your disposal at this very moment. You, right now, have within you everything you need to begin creating a better life for yourself and for those around you.

So where do you begin? The first thing you need to know is this: *Turning the Page in life is a choice.* It is a choice to position yourself to achieve your dreams. You don't just wake up and find yourself successful. You don't just open your eyes one day and find yourself fulfilled. In order to qualify for it, you have to make a choice, and the question you have to ask yourself is, "what kinds of things must I commit to, and what kind of things must be cut off from my life?" What must I commit to, and what must I cut off?

Robert Frost, the poet, answered that question for us when he penned the following words:

Two roads diverged in a wood, and I—
I took the one less traveled by,
And that has made all the difference.

Walking through the woods on a winding road, under the spreading sunrise, the poet, Robert Frost, came to a fork in the road. He slowed down to think about which of the two roads he should take. One of the roads had on it smashed shrubbery, flattened clumps of grass, and a trampled carpet of wildflowers, because many people had traveled down that road.

I imagine that the other road was robustly green, and had on it clinging gardens, shrubs and low vegetation. The road was dotted with rocks, enclosed with hills. That road was un-cultivated and un-peopled. Compared with the first road, few people had gone down that second road. As such, the second road was the road "less traveled."

Rather than taking the well-worn, grass-trampled road, Robert Frost chose, in his own life, to walk down the road "less traveled." He concludes the poem by saying that his choice to take the less-traveled road had made all the difference in his life.

In the same way, you and I are presented with two roads every day. We can choose the road that most people walk on, or we can choose a path that very few people take. The first road is filled with people who are following the crowd, and who accept mediocrity, being average, and fitting in. It is a road that is filled with people who have decided to settle for "good enough."

However, the second road—the road with all the shrubs and vegetation—is a road that leads to greatness. It is the road to success, the road to self-realization, the road to living your dreams. The second road has very little traffic. If you take the second road, you will be lonely at times, because you may have to separate yourself (cut yourself off) from people who do not believe in you.

Turning the page (working to create the life of your dreams) is the "road less traveled," because few people actually make the decision to walk down that road. The road less traveled requires you to leave your comfort zone, and do some things to position yourself for success.

Success begins with the desire for more in life, and turning the page (making a choice—a decision—to achieve those dreams and desires). I'll say it again: success is not something that just happens to you; it is a choice you must make.

So, what's the first choice you should make, right now? The choice to TURN THE PAGE! Are you behind on your bills or broke? Good! Turn the page, right now! Are you fat and frustrated? Good! Turn the page, right now! Do others underestimate you and your abilities? Good! Are you overworked and underpaid? Good! Do members of the opposite sex keep putting you in the "friend zone"? Good! Turn the page, right now! Do people think you are a joke or a loser? Good! Turn the page, right now! Pain, pressure, and problems are signs that you're about to make some good changes in your life. Pain and frustration can be a great motivator, a meaningful inspiration, and a powerful impetus for turning the page.

I want you to deal with your problems by turning the page. Take responsibility for your life. Right now. Stop waiting for your parents to fix your situation. Stop waiting for your boss to make your life better. Stop hoping for someone of the opposite sex to make your life better? No! You turn the page! You decide. You commit to achieving the kind of life that you want. You cut off those things that are holding you back. Right now.

ASSIGNMENT #2
ONE DECISION

What is one thing you have been putting off that you can get done right now? You need to put your Turning the Page decision-making power to work right away. Pick one thing right now, and commit to getting it done immediately. Pick one thing you know you need to do, but have not yet done it. Then, go do it. Get it done. Turn the page! Right now!

CHAPTER 3
YOUR FOUNDATION

The tallest building in the world, Burj Khalifa ("Khalifa Tower"), stands 2,722 feet above the ground. It's so tall that you can see it from 60 miles away. It took 22 million man-hours to build. When people look at the building, they admire its beauty and splendor. They admire its breathtaking heights, and gargantuan stature. What most people don't realize is that 330,000 tons of concrete and steel were used to build it, and that 110,000 of those tons are 164 feet below the ground. That's right, the foundation for the whole building makes up one-third of the entire structure. *33% of the entire building is below the ground.* In order to ensure that such a tall building would not twist or break when storms raged and winds blew, the builders made sure to build it upon a solid, reliable foundation. That foundation is what keeps the building from being overtaken by nature's power. That foundation is what keeps it from falling over.

In the same way, if you want to rise to towering heights in your life, you must make sure that you build your life on a sure, solid foundation. The foundations upon which you build your life determine how high you can rise. You must make sure to lay the proper foundation.

Because foundations are unseen, they often go unappreciated. People don't get to see you doing the hard work of excavating the soil of your soul, and laying the groundwork, and pouring in the concrete, and laying the steel beams; all they see is the end result. They don't see the sweat on your brow, the blood on your knuckles, or the ache in your bones; all they see are the victories, and the trophies, and the money and the things—the end result. People always admire the end result; they hardly ever appreciate the foundation upon which that masterpiece stands. Nevertheless, if you are going to build a great life, or write a great new chapter in your life, you must make sure you have a solid foundation.

If, however, tragedy does strike and the storms of life knock you down, you can always build again as long as you have laid the proper foundation. You can always start over, and build another masterpiece, as long as you have a solid, sure foundation. On the contrary, if you do not have a solid foundation, nothing you build upon it will last very long. Nothing you build on it can withstand any struggles or storms. As soon as something opposes it, it will crumble. It will fall. Because its foundation was weak.

However, if you have the right foundation, you can plant and grow a successful, multi-million dollar business; and, even if you lost millions of dollars, you could make back all the money you lost. Why? Because you have built your life upon the right foundation. You have the right stuff that is beneath the surface.

In this chapter I'm going to share with you the foundational principles upon which my life is built, and the foundational principles upon which you would do well to build your own life. Upon these basic principles you can build anything of consequence. Upon these principles, you can build a life that will stand the test of time. Upon these truths, you can be confident that the life you want to create for yourself will endure even the most terrible storms.

FAITH

In life, some events, and people, are going to knock you down. People are going to try to discourage you. Sometimes fear is going to try to cripple you, and scare you. Fear will try to talk you out of some things, and tell you that you are not smart enough, or good enough, or deserving enough. Fear will rob you of your power to improve your life. It will keep you from taking risks on yourself, and it will keep you from realizing your dreams. That's why I believe it is absolutely imperative for you to have faith as a part of your life's foundation.

What is faith? I will discuss it a little more later on, but for now, you need to understand that faith is the substance of things hoped for. That means that you believe in something so much that you can almost touch it, smell it, feel, or taste it. Having faith is being able to "experience" something in your mind before you actually touch it with your hands. To have faith means you see something with your "spiritual" eye that is currently invisible to the "natural" eye. Faith is what you need to turn your mental vision into its physical equivalent. Faith is what you will need to turn your dreams into reality.

I would not be who I am and where I am in life if it were not for my faith that things in my life were going to get better. In many of my most difficult moments in life, I had that special something, that deep down belief, that I was going to make it through those tough times. Faith is what keeps you sane when everything around you seems to be falling apart. Faith is what inspires you to keep pressing foreword when everyone else has given up. Faith is what tells you, that no matter how hard things are right now, "this too shall pass."

LOVE

You would also do well to base your life on love. The world is filled with hate, and meanness. People and things will work hard to make you an angry, abusive, and bitter person. People will be jealous of you, and try to sabotage your success, and even try to take your place. Those kinds of experiences will try to steal your joy, and make you mean and maniacal. If you let them, those people and things will ruin your life. But, if you are ever going to make it to your desired destination in life, I'm absolutely convinced that you must let love be a central part of your daily life.

The Greek language comes to our aid when talking about love. In Greek, there are several words used to describe love. First, there is *eros* love, which refers to a kind of romantic, erotic love. It is the kind of love that you have when you are attracted to someone else. This love is wonderful, but it is in-complete, because it is a selfish kind of love. It is a kind of love that causes you to be attracted to someone else because of what you think they can do *for you*.

Then there is *phileo* love, which refers to a kind of brotherly love. The city of Philadelphia (phileo= brotherly love + adelphos= brother) is called the city of brotherly love because of this word. Brotherly, or sisterly, love is the kind of love that you have for someone who is a friend. You enjoy being around that person. You probably have similar interests, and have a lot in common. His love, as great as it is, is still inadequate, because it too is a little self-serving. You love someone else because of how they make you feel. You love someone else because you enjoy being around them, and they enjoy being around you. While there is nothing wrong with that, it is still incomplete, because your love is still based upon how that person makes *you* feel.

Third, there is *agape* love. Agape refers to a kind of self-less love. Agape is a kind of unconditional love. It is the kind of love that causes you to do for others, even if it hurts you. Agape love is the kind of love that causes you to sacrifice your own comfort, your own well-being, your own pleasure, for the sake of someone else. This kind of love is the most powerful force in the world. There is nothing else like it. This kind of love is the kind of love that I encourage you to base your life on, for this kind of love has a way of making the world a better place, and simultaneously helping you grow as a person.

Because agape love is the most powerful force in all the world, and I encourage you to greet each day with love in your heart. I encourage you to not only love yourself, for you are beautiful, you matter, you are not an accident, and you are here for a reason; but, I also encourage you to love others, for you might just encourage someone's heart, change someone's per-spective, or even save someone's life.

GRATITUDE

We live in an age when people are becoming increasingly entitled. They feel as though they are entitled to special privileges and attention. It seems like people are becoming more self-centered, and spoiled. Consequently, when things don't go their way, they tend to overreact, or blow things out of proportion, and throw temper tantrums. People like that are never satisfied. They always feel entitled to more. They always believe that they *deserve* something bigger, and better than others. They go through life believing that they should start off where others are ending up in life. They don't realize that people who have nice things usually had to work hard for those things, and have sacrificed in order to get those things. As a result of this sense of entitlement, many people have the worst, most ungrateful attitudes.

There was a woman, let's call her Sue, who worked at the customer service desk at the Kalahari Resorts in the Wisconsin Dells. Sue sat behind a desk and tried to help people who needed some kind of assistance. The day I was there with my family, it seemed like everyone who was going to Sue was upset about something related to the hotel. Some people were even raising their voices at her. Despite their rudeness, Sue remained calm, and tried to help them.

When Sue had helped everyone else, I approached her counter. She looked at me with warm, smiling eyes, and said, "Hello, sir. How may I help you today?"

Impressed, I said to her, "You handled all those people so well. The way you kept you cool was great."

She smiled and responded, "Thanks. A lot of people seem to overreact about the smallest things, and I try to help them as much as I can." She then told me a story about one of the resort's residents who had approached her in a panic. The lady apparently had lost her diamond earring in the hotel room, and was nearly hyperventilating.

Sue did everything in her power to locate the woman's earring. She contacted lost and found, she talked with the hotel's manager, but could not find the woman's earring. The woman who lost the earring was still not satisfied, and became even more irate. Sue, having done all she could do, looked at the woman and said, "ma'am, it's an earring. An earring. I'm so sorry that I can't do more to help you find it; but I'm pretty sure you're going to be fine."

The lady was taken aback by Sue's nonchalant attitude about such an expensive, diamond earring. After all, it was a diamond earring she lost. Offended, the woman crossed her arms, and said, "I beg your pardon!"

Sue said, "I looked at her as calmly as I could, and said again, 'Ma'am, you're going to be fine without your earring. It's just an earring. ... My son died yesterday. He died. ... I'm pretty sure you're going to be just fine without your earring.'"

After hearing that, Sue said the woman's whole posture changed. She instantly apologized for her behavior and expressed her condolences Sue's loss. The woman said, "I'm so sorry. I'm so sorry for your loss. You're right. I'm going to be just fine without my earring." She then walked away with a whole new attitude.

Now, I too would probably be upset if I had lost something

as expensive as a diamond earring. However, Sue's story is a great reminder to keep your problems in perspective. Always remember that no matter how bad things are for you, they could always be worse. Be grateful for what you have in your life. Be grateful for your life; be grateful for your health; be grateful for your mind; be grateful for the food and water you get; be grateful for those who love you and those you love; be grateful for the little things. Don't grieve over what you've lost; be grateful for what you have left. Things could always be worse. In your next chapter, always try to find time to give thanks for the good things that are going on in your life. Give thanks daily.

HUMILITY

I also believe that humility will take you a long way in life. There are a lot of people who feel as though they need to tell the world about how great they are. They toot their own horns, and sing their own praises. They are boastful and arrogant. While I don't think anything is wrong with presenting your best-self to world by telling others about your accomplishments, I do think you ought to be very careful about how you do so, for you could come off as arrogant and boastful. Confidence is one thing; arrogance is something totally different.

To be boastful refers to what you say, to be arrogant refers to how you behave. They are two sides of the same coin. Boasting is arrogance of speech, bluster, exaggerated superfluity, unbridled loquacity. Boasting is baseless chatter, and it is rooted in pride. It is rooted in you trying to make yourself look better than other people. It is rooted in a desire to impress someone.

Arrogance causes a person to boast. Arrogance is having exaggerated concept of yourself. Arrogance is really a combination of ego and ignorance, and often rooted in insecurity. The most arrogant, boastful, proud people I have met are also the most insecure. They boast about how great they are, or how much money they have, or about how many fine and luxurious things they own. Deep down, they want others to accept them; and, they really want to accept themselves. Boastful people often want others to approve of them, or affirm them as people. I'll come back to this topic later in the book, but for now, I just want you to see that you when you have self-confidence, and a sense of security about yourself, you don't need to receive the affirmation or adulation of other people.

Instead, I believe that you should let your speech be filled with grace, and your words be seasoned with humility. Rather than trying to impress other people with how great you think you are (or how great you want them to think you are), humble yourself, and live your life so well that your life speaks for itself. That kind of life inspires others to recognize and appreciate your worth. Don't puff yourself up, but let others give you your props. It's tasteless to praise yourself anyway.

INTEGRITY

The word integrity means "whole, entire, complete, all there." In our English language, integrity is derived from a cognate word, integer. In math, integer is a term you use for whole numbers, not fractions. So 1, 2, 3, 4 are integers; 1/2, 2/4, and 3/4 are fractions. An integer is not a half, it's not a slice, it's not a slit—it's the whole thing. And so to have integrity means not to let even a tiny slice be cut away from you to be used for doing wrong. To have integrity means refusing to let even a small slice of you be involved in that which is wrong, that which is inappropriate. To have integrity means you are living your life in a way that is not inconsistent with what you believe and what you profess to believe.

Let me try to explain this another way. *USA Today* reported in their April 9, 1997, edition that scientists now say that a series of slits, not a giant gash, sank the *Titanic.* The opulent, 900-foot cruise ship sank in 1912 on its first voyage, from England to New York, and fifteen hundred people died.

The most widely held theory was that the ship hit an iceberg, which opened a huge gash in the side of the liner. But an international team of divers and scientists recently used sound waves to probe the wreckage, which is buried in the mud under two-and-a-half miles of water. What did these divers and scientists find? The damage was surprisingly small. Instead of the huge gash, they found some small, narrow slits along the bottom of the ship.

In the same way, just as small slits, small slices, invisible to most, can sink a great ship, small slits, and small slices in your character, which most people can't see, can sink your character. Telling a white lie, that's a slit; flirting with a married man or woman, that's a slit; lying on your taxes, that's a slit; stealing resources from your job, no matter how small, that's a slit; showing up late even though you knew what time you were supposed to be there, and making up an excuse for your absence, that's a slit; blaming others for your shortcomings, that's a slit; gossiping about others, that's a slit; cheating on your exams, that's a slit. I'm not talking about accidental slits; I'm talking about character flaws that you can repair. I'm talking about slits you can fix.

When I was working on my instrument rating for my pilot's certificate (a rating that allows me to fly through clouds), I spent a great deal of time with my Senior Flight Instructor, Blane "Eric" Bergson. Eric is not only a pilot, but is also a mechanic who can fix and build airplanes. He can also install avionics. He is an encyclopedia of knowledge and wisdom when it comes to anything related to aviation. For nearly two weeks straight, Eric and I spent nearly ten to twelve hours a day talking about airplanes and aviation.

There were many times when I wanted to end our sessions early because I was tired, but he insisted that we not cut our days short. He explained, "Manny, everything I am telling you has been written in blood. People died for us to learn these things. I need to tell you what people did that killed them. Why what they did was wrong. Then I am going to tell you the right way to do it, so that, when you get into those situations, you don't kill yourself. I've been flying for 35 years, and I've trained hundreds of students, and not one of them has ever died in a plane crash. One of these days you are going to come to me, and you are going to thank me for saving your life. It has already happened several times. So we need to take the full ten or twelve hours every day to make sure you really learn this stuff." Despite my desires to cut my training-days short, Eric refused because too much was at stake (my life!).

Eric is a man of integrity. Because he did what was in my best interests, I would send my own wife and children to him with a blank check so he could teach them how to fly. I know that Eric would not take advantage of them, and I know that he would train them to be safe, smart pilots. When it came to training, Eric had no "slits." He was complete, the real deal.

In this next chapter of your life, it's important for you to eliminate the slits in your life. It's important for you to be a person of integrity.

HONESTY

Related to integrity is honesty. It seems like we are living in a time when more and more people think it is okay to lie. Some people define a lie as a "very present help in the time of trouble." A lie would make no sense unless the truth were felt to be dangerous. Because of this lack of honesty in our world, fewer and fewer people trust one another. People tell white lies and think it's okay. People lie to their friends and loved ones about their outfits, their significant others, and all kinds of stuff.

However, if your next chapter is going to be great, I believe you have to commit to being honest with yourself about everything. Truth is true even if nobody believes it, and falsehood is false even if everyone believes it. Because of that, I have always tried to be brutally honest with myself. When I have blown it, I admit it. I own my mistakes. When I have missed the mark, I admit that I fell short. It's my honesty that has allowed me to correct my mistakes and get better. In the same way, I believe that you should develop the habit of being honest with yourself.

I also think you should be honest with other people. People often say they want people to tell them the truth, but as soon as someone gives what they ask for, they get upset. I'm convinced that most people do not like to hear to truth about themselves. Be that as it may, I believe that you shall know the truth, and the truth shall set you free. To be sure, I don't believe you need to tell everybody everything that's on your mind, especially if they did not ask you for your advice. However, when the opportunity presents itself, or because someone is about to do something that could ruin their lives, I believe you should speak your mind, even if your voice shakes.

Tell the truth even if it makes you unpopular; tell the truth if it makes you uncomfortable; tell the truth. ... In the grand scheme of your story, I believe that it will serve you, and others, well.

SELF-DISCIPLINE

Finally, commit to being self-disciplined. If you are going to achieve anything great in life, you are going to have to discipline yourself. You must gain mastery over your time, your mind, and your body. The most successful people discipline their minds and bodies to achieve great things. Success is not about doing what feels good. It's easy to do things that you enjoy doing; but to be great, you are going to have to do a whole lot of things that you do not enjoy doing. You are going to have to do some things that you just hate. Things that don't feel good; but, things that are nonetheless necessary if you are going to be great. Discipline involves sacrifice, it involves discomfort; it involves pain. But, in the end, it is worth it, because it leads to great rewards.

As I end this chapter, I want to tell you about a man who bought a new house. After he moved in, he noticed that there were a few cracks on the walls. So he bought some paint, and painted over the cracks. A few days later, he noticed some more cracks on the walls, and painted over the cracks again. A few days later, he was walking through his living room, and he saw even more cracks on the walls.

He became frustrated, and called an inspector to help him with the problem. The inspector walked around the house, and came back to the owner of the house and said, "sir, you don't have any problems with your walls." And the owner, irritated by the inspector's assessment, responded, "Yes, I do have a problem." The inspector said, "No, you don't." And the owner said, "Yes, I do!" The inspector said, "No, sir, you don't." The owner, being unable to contain himself anymore, grabbed the inspector by the arm, pulled him over to the wall, pointed at the cracks, and, with obvious frustration in his voice, the owner says emphatically, "Yes, I do have a problem with my walls!" The inspector finally says, "Sir, you do not have a problem with your walls! The problem is that your house is built on a moving foundation. Your house is on unstable ground, and whenever it moves, your walls crack."

A lot of people have cracks on the walls of their lives, and constantly try to cover those cracks with a quick fix. The problem is, if they have not built their lives upon a sure, stable foundation, more cracks are going to keep showing up in their lives.

If you want to have a life that is free of cracks, make sure to build it on the foundation of faith, love, gratitude, humility, integrity, honesty, and self-discipline. Doing so can help the next chapters of your life be so much more stable, fulfilling and satisfying.

ASSIGNMENT #3
YOUR FOUNDATION

Take an assessment of your life right now. How are you do-
ing in these seven areas? How strong is your faith? Your love?
Your humility? Your gratitude? Your integrity? Your honesty?
Your self-discipline?

CHAPTER 4

YOUR DREAMS

She was a young lady who was born blind, deaf, and mute; she could not speak, she could not hear, and she could not see. However, with a fierce tenacity, an unwavering determination, and unrelenting vigor, Helen Keller learned how to read, write, and communicate very well. After thinking about her own condition, and the obstacles she had overcome, she said that *"Worse than being blind is to see but have no vision."*

Too many people can see but they have no vision, or no dreams. Too many people are just coasting through life, from pillar to post, going here and there, without any clear direction. This kind of wandering is merely a symptom of not having vision or a dream.

Dreams, more than anything else, affect the attitudes you have, the actions you take, and the decisions you make. Every day, your dreams determine how you spend your time, who you spend it with, and what you spend it on.

In this chapter, you will learn what a dream or vision is, why it is so important for you to have one, and how you can discover it, so that you can translate those dreams or visions into reality. In this chapter, I will refer to dreams and visions as synonyms because, in this context, they refer to essentially the same thing.

WHAT IS A DREAM?

A dream is a mental picture about your near or distant future. Let me break that down for you. Your *reality* is where you are *right now*. Your reality is the set of circumstances, state-of-affairs, or conditions that you are living with right now. However, your dream is the set of circumstances, state-of-affairs, or conditions that you see yourself having in your near or immediate *future*. ***A dream—a clear mental picture of your near or distant future—gives you the ability to see beyond your present realities, and to become what you not yet are.***

For example, your reality may be that you are living in a rented, cramped apartment, fighting over one bathroom, and arguing over who gets the remote control. Your dream, however, may be own a nice, big home, with several bathrooms, a swimming pool, and a theater, and a game room. You dream allows you to see yourself in your new home.

Your reality may be that you work on a job where you are not fulfilled, your supervisor is unfair, your pay is low, and your responsibilities are overwhelming; but your dream may be to own your own business, where you are the boss, and you love what you do. Your dream allows you to see yourself starting and growing your own business.

Your reality may be that you are a shy, soft-spoken person who hates public speaking; but your dream may be to become a confident, well-spoken, eloquent person who has mastered the English language. Your dream allows you to see yourself speaking to people with fluidity and confidence.

Your reality may be that you are single, saving yourself for marriage, and refusing to settle for just anybody; but your dream may be to be in a loving, fulfilling, covenant relationship, with someone who is willing to give to you just as much as you are willing to give to him or her. Your dream allows you to see yourself walking on the beach, holding hands with that person.

Again, your reality is the current set of circumstances, states-of-affairs, or actual conditions that you are facing right now; your dream is what you see yourself becoming, the circumstances you see yourself having, the income that you see yourself making, the lifestyle that you see yourself enjoying, the kind of person you see yourself becoming. That's what dreams are made of. The ability to see, and become, what you not yet are.

Let me pause here and ask you, what is your dream? What mental picture do you have in your head about your immediate or distant future? What do you see in your future that takes you beyond your present reality, your current state of affairs, your current conditions? What picture do you see about where you are going, what you are going to become, what you are going to possess, what you are going to enjoy, what you are going to share, what you are going to distribute, what you are going to do? What is your vision? What is your dream? What is your hope? What inspires you, what wakes you up in the morning? What gives you an energy boost when you think about it? What would you do for free because you love it? If you could not fail, what would you do with your life? What is your dream? Where would you love to vacation? Where would you love to go to school? Where do you want to open that business? Where would you love to shop? Who would you love to help? What problems would you love to solve? What societal needs would you love to meet? What is your vision? What is your dream?

DREAMS GIVES YOU HOPE

Why is having a dream or vision so important? Because if you don't have a dream, then you are stuck with your reality. You are trapped by your current situation. Without a dream, you are smothered by your current state of affairs. Without a dream, all you have is now; and, if your current situation—your now—is not that great, then you are going to be miserable. Your now, if it is as hard as my "now" used to be, can be suffocating.

If all you have is your reality—and your reality is hard—then you are going to be depressed. When you dwell on your reality, you are likely to take up drinking, drugs, violence, or some other coping mechanism. When all you have is your now—your reality—then you have nothing to motivate you.

Without a dream, you just go to your job, and do the bare minimum. Without a dream, you just go to school because everyone says you have to, but never really enjoy it. Without a dream that your marriage can get better, you just go through the motions, and have a meaningless, boring relationship. Without a dream, you are more likely to settle for second-best. You accept mediocrity. You become complacent.

However, when you get a dream or vision for your life, you get a glimpse of *what can be. You get a glimpse of your own possibilities.* Vision, as such, gives you a mental picture about your future, which then gives you hope. By giving you hope, vision motivates you, encourages you, and propels you forward. Sometimes, a dream is all you have to keep you going in the midst of your reality. Dreams, after you have been crying all night, are the only thing that keep you getting up in the morning. Dreams, after you have been knocked down by heartbreak and disappointment, is what inspires you to get up and try again. Dreams allow you see yourself as you *will be* even though you *not yet* are that person. Dreams, because they are so powerful, give you hope.

DREAMS GIVE YOU DIRECTION

Why else is having a dream or vision so important? Stephen Covey says in his book, *First Things First*, that "[v]ision can become a motivating force so powerful it becomes the DNA of your life. It's so ingrained and integrated into every aspect of your being that it becomes the compelling impetus behind every decision we make. It's the fire within—the explosion of inner synergy that happens … It's the energy that makes life an adventure—the deep burning 'yes!' that empowers us to say "no"—peacefully and confidently—to the less important things in our lives."

When you have a vision for your life, you get a sense of direction. It gives you clarity about where you are going, and how you are going to get there, and what it's going to take for you to get there. When you have a vision, you are empowered to say "no" to the less important things in your life, so that you can focus on things that can put you one step closer to your dreams.

Without a vision, your life will be scattered. I read a Hebrew proverb, which says, "Where there is no vision, people get out of hand."

The phrase "get out of hand," in the Hebrew language, often refers to hair that is hanging loose without a turban, or in modern terms, a "head-wrap" or a "wave-cap." Have you ever seen how a woman's hair looks when she has gone to bed without wrapping or rolling her hair the night before? Regardless of her attempt the next morning to style it, it goes in all kinds of directions, doing whatever it wants to do. It looks like it needs conditioner, a retouch, and a miracle.

What I am trying to say is that your life without vision is like hair without a head-wrap—it is all over the place. It's messy, it's not cute; it ain't pretty; it's out of control; and, it's in need of a miracle. Without vision, your life is all over the place.

On the contrary, by inference, life *with* vision is like hair that has had a head-wrap the night before. It is controlled, it is contained, it is trained, and it is going in the same direction. Life with vision is like hair with a wave cap. The hair is wavy, going in the same direction.

The first semester of my freshman year in high school, I earned an "F" in Jazz, a "C" in English, a "D" in World History, a "D" in Physical Education, a "D" in Band, an "F" in Spanish, and an "F" in Math. I think that averages out to a 0.6 Grade Point Average! If one were to predict what kind of future I would have based on these grades, I have no doubt that the forecast would be grim. My grades were terrible. My second semester grades weren't that much better—I dropped out of high school!

I went back to school that following year, and my first semester back, I earned an "A" in Math, an "A" in Drivers Ed., a "B" in English, an "A" in Physical Education, an "A" in Career Guidance, a "B" in Graphic Arts, and an "A" in Life Science.

What happened? How did I go from being an "F" student, to an "A" student? How did I go from being un-teachable to academically unstoppable?

I saw a brighter future for myself.

After I dropped out of high school, a man named Martin helped me turn my life around. He helped me see beyond my present circumstances, and get a glimpse of a brighter future for myself. That vision, that dream, that hope, that glimpse, inspired me to make the decision to change.

What was my vision? It was a vision of me breaking the cycle of poverty and pain in my family. It was a vision of me graduating from high school. It was a vision of me creating a better life for myself and those I love. It was the vision of me one day owning a home, and being the kind of father that I never had. It was a vision of me empowering others, and giving people hope. That vision literally woke me from my slumber, and inspired me to make big changes in my life.

DREAMS REQUIRE FAITH

If you don't have a vision or dream, then you have no hope. In other words, you are not hoping for anything if you don't have a dream or a vision of a better future for yourself. If you are not hoping for anything, then you don't need to have faith.

Let me explain the connection between your reality, vision/ dream, hope, and faith. What is faith? Faith is the substance of things hoped for. That means that you believe in something so much that you can almost touch, smell it, feel, or taste it. Having faith is being able to "experience" something in your mind before you actually "experience" it with your hands. To have faith means you see something with your "spiritual" eye that is currently invisible to the "natural" eye. Faith is what you need to turn your mental vision into its physical equivalent.

Reality is where you are right now; and, as I have already said, vision is where you see yourself being in the future. Hope is the longing you have in your heart to have that which you see in your future through your vision or dream. And, faith tells you that it is only a matter of time before your vision becomes your reality.

Faith is the substance of things hoped for. In other words, vision is the picture in your head and heart that you hope becomes reality; faith is the substance of that hope. Faith lets you almost touch, smell, or taste the picture you are hoping for in your head and heart. Faith gives you the substance in your head and heart before you ever touch it with your hands.

Enough of all that mumbo-jumbo. How does all of this work in real life? When I was still a young man in high school, when I was still learning the basics of English grammar—long before I became a public speaker—I saw visions of myself standing before large groups of people, inspiring them with words that I was speaking. Sometimes, when I heard other speakers make presentations during assemblies, I often saw myself delivering my own message in their place.

The same thing happened to me in college, at the University of California at Berkeley. Because of these visions of myself speaking to large crowds, I often mentally transformed my little bedroom into a coliseum where an old upright speaker became my lectern, and all the objects in my room became my audience. For hours I would recite poetry and speeches in my empty room.

During college, I worked for pennies as a Loss Prevention Specialist—just a fancy name for security guard. It was my job to secure the buildings by making sure all the doors were locked, the lights were off, and the place was empty. Many nights, after all the buildings were secure, I went to the largest ballroom in the building (Pauley Ballroom), and for hours, I recited speeches to an empty room. Eventually, I found myself doing that in the largest venues on campus (such as Wheeler Auditorium), which sat over seven hundred people. I even found a way to practice a few times on the platform of the eighty-five-hundred-seat Hearst Greek Theater. Even though each venue was empty, in my mind, I was speaking to a standing room only crowd of people who were being inspired by my words. I would speak as though the room were packed to capacity with people who needed to hear what I had to say. I would speak, inspiring thousands, painting for them a vision of a brighter tomorrow. I would speak, telling people that in spite of where they come from, they can achieve their dreams. I would speak, and I would see, in my head, lives being changed.

Mentally, emotionally, and behaviorally I was committed to making that dream a reality. I started reading books about speaking, and studying some of the world's most powerful speakers. When I went to sleep, I had dreams about speaking, and, in my dreams, I saw lives being changed. I saw people being moved by my words. You could not tell me that those dreams were not real, because everything about them affected my body physically. Sometimes I would wake up from those dreams and I would be sweating. Sometimes my heart would be racing. In those dreams, I had conversations with my role models. In my dreams, I remember walking around with the Rev. Dr. Martin Luther King Jr. I would watch him, and listen to him, and learn from him … in my dreams. I saw Frederick Douglass, and others, close up, in my dreams. I saw myself speaking before audiences, in my dreams. As I write these words, my heart is beginning to speed up, because I remember those dreams so vividly.

Around that time, people began to invite me to be the master of ceremonies for campus events. I became the guy who was on the microphone engaging, entertaining, and empowering audiences, young and old. Shortly after that, I began receiving invitations at speak to elementary and middle school students. Then I began receiving invitations to speak to high school students. Before long, I began receiving invitations to speak to community organizations. Eventually, I began receiving invitations to speak in other states. Finally, I began to receive invitations to speak in other countries.

I absolutely love what I do. When nobody else believed in me, I had dreams that inspired me. I had a vision for my life that caused me to fall in love with books. Those dreams inspired me to want to learn how to summon the English language and send it into battle. In a small room, with a speaker box, all I had was a dream of inspiring people with my words. That small bedroom at 554 Liberty Street, in El Cerrito, California, led me to an empty ballroom; that empty ballroom led me filled classrooms; those classrooms led me to speak in filled ballrooms; those ballrooms have opened doors for me to speak at filled convention centers. A little while ago, I had the privilege of speaking in Hong Kong, China, to a Coliseum of twelve thousand people who had traveled from one hundred and ninety-two countries. And, shortly after that, I spoke to a crowd of 100,000 people.

The young man who seemed to have every disadvantage, who was classified as an ESL student; who had a 0.6 G.P.A.; and, who was a high school dropout, now has the privilege of speaking to hundreds of thousands of people a year. Whether I'm in Houston or Hong Kong, Kansas City or Cairo, Los Angeles or London, I love carrying the torchlight of hope into the recesses of dormant potential, and showing the gems that are sparkling there.

But don't miss this: *It all began as a dream! It started as a vision. It started as something that only existed in my head and heart. My faith that my dream could become a part of my daily reality changed my life.*

Your dreams, joined with your faith, have the power to change your life too!

SO, WHAT DO YOU REALLY WANT OUT OF LIFE?

Dennis Kimbro, in *Think and Grow Rich*, talks about the secret of success. He tells of an old African sage, who was wise and influential, and who lived on the side of a mountain near a lake. It was common practice for the people of the village to seek his advice. The old man spent many hours sitting in front of his small hut, where he rocked in a crude rocking chair made of branches and twigs. Hour after hour, he sat and rocked as he thought.

One day he noticed a young African warrior walking on the path toward his hut. The young man walked up the hill and stood erect before the sage. "What can I do for you?" the old man said.

The warrior replied, "I was told by those in the village that you are very wise. They said that you could give me the secret of happiness and the good life."

The old man listened, then gazed at the ground for several moments. He rose to his feet, took the boy by the hand, and led him down the path back toward the lake. Not a word was spoken. The young warrior was obviously bewildered, but the sage kept walking. Soon they approached the lake, but did not stop. Out into the water, the old man led the boy. The farther they walked, the higher the water advanced. The water rose from the boy's knees to his waist, then to his chin, but the old man said nothing and kept moving deeper and deeper. Finally the lad was completely submerged. At this point the wise man stopped for a moment, turned the boy around, and led him out of the lake and up the path back to the hut. Still not a word was spoken. The old man sat again in his creaky chair and rocked to and fro.

After several thought-provoking minutes, he looked into the boy's questioning eyes and asked, "young man, when you were in the lake, underwater, what was it you desired most?"

Openly excited, the boy replied, "Why, you old fool, I wanted to breathe!"

Then the sage spoke these words: "My son, when you want happiness in life as badly as you wanted to breathe, you will have found the secret."

I share that story with you to ask you a question: What do you really want in life? What do you really desire? What are you hungry for? What is that thing in your heart that you long for? Or, put another way, what is your dream? When you get clear about what you really want, and you want it as much as you want to breath, then that dream has a much better chance of becoming your reality.

ASSIGNMENT #4
YOUR DREAMS

At the risk of being redundant, if you want to achieve your dreams, you need to first get clear about your them. You need to "detect" or "discover" them by asking yourself, "where do I want to end up in life?"

The following questions are designed to help you discover what your future could be like. You definitely need to take time to write out your answers in your own private notebook or journal, because writing just does something to your mind and heart. It commits you to having something more than wishful thinking. Writing things down tells your mind and heart that you are serious about something. Get to writing, so you can catch a glimpse of your own possibilities!

I have listed some of my own dreams on the following page.

DREAM
I dream of myself traveling, speaking to people around the world, inspiring and equipping others to overcome their obstacles and achieve their dreams.
I dream of myself being a faithful, loyal husband to my wife.
I dream of being a loving father to my children.
I dream of being healthy in every area of my life: mentally, emotionally, spiritually, physically, and financially.
I dream of learning to fly airplanes.
I dream of owning my own home.
I dream of being financially free.

WRITE DOWN YOUR OWN DREAMS

If money were not an issue, what would you do for free? What do you enjoy doing most? What brings you the most joy? Your answer to these questions might be a clue to help you discover what your dreams are.

Do you love to travel, sing, write, read, teach, preach, dance, or build? Do you like to debate, research, or do experiments? Do you like to play the piano, style hair, design clothes, or handle money? Do you like working on cars, business, or furniture? Think about it, and write down whatever comes to your mind.

Or, what gets on your last nerve? What burdens you? Does disorganization, ineffective programs, inhospitality, irrelevant preaching, or bad music upset you? Your answer to these questions might give you a clue as to what your vision, dream, or calling in life might be. For example, if you get bothered whenever you hear a band playing music poorly, then you might be wired to be involved in music of some sort. If you absolutely abhor it when things are disorganized, you might be wired to be a project manager or planner of some sort. If your heart is pierced with grief and compassion whenever you see homeless people, then you might be a social justice advocate or something like that.

Also, what abilities do you have that others have complimented or affirmed? What can you do better than others? What sets you apart? What unique skills do you have that you can use with very little effort? Are you naturally good at using computers, making music, typing, or negotiation?

Also, what is your temperament or personality-type? Have you taken the DISC, Myers-Briggs, or some other personality analysis? Are you a dominant person, an influencer, a supporter, or a compliant person? In other words, do you care more about getting things done than you do about people's feelings? Or do you care more about how people feel than you do about getting things done? Are you a behind the scenes person who just wants to help where there is a need? Or, are you a person who is very detail-oriented, and needs to plan for every little thing before you make a decision? You should really take one of these assessments if you haven't already done so, because they help you understand yourself, and they help you see how you tend to relate to others. Such personality assessments also help you understand how to improve the way in which you communicate with others.

Finally, what experience do you have that might help you get a glimpse of your future? What experiences have you had personally, what jobs have you had, what challenges have you faced or conquered which shaped who you are? For example, many women who have been abused would probably be able to counsel and assist others who have been abused. Also, people who have been homeless have a unique way of understanding and relating to homeless people. As such, they might have a vision, dream, or calling to find housing for the homeless.

These are just some questions to help you think about the big picture of your life. Remember, all things have two creations: first things are created in our minds, and then they are created in reality. Therefore, turn the page, and take matters into your own hands, and begin figuring out what your dream, vision, or calling is.

Whatever your dreams are, list them in the tables on the next pages, or in your journal. I have included more space for you just in case you have more dreams. I have given you seven areas for you to consider your dreams.

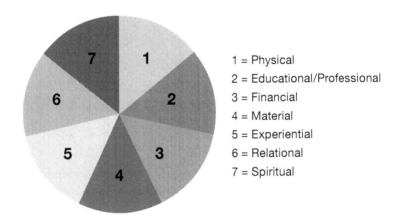

1 = Physical
2 = Educational/Professional
3 = Financial
4 = Material
5 = Experiential
6 = Relational
7 = Spiritual

What are your physical dreams? How much do you want to weigh? How do you want your body to look? Do you want ripped abs? Do you want to be able to run a four-minute mile? Do 70 push-ups in 60 seconds? Be able to run in a marathon? What are your physical goals? Write them in the space below.

YOUR PHYSICAL DREAMS

What are your dreams for school? Do you want to be the first in your family to graduate from college? Do you want to earn a doctorate? What are you vocational or professional goals? Do you want to own your own company? Be the president or CEO? Plant and grow a ministry? Write them in the space below.

YOUR EDUCATIONAL/PROFESSIONAL DREAMS

What are your financial goals? How much money would you like to earn an hour? A day? A week? A month? A year? How much money would you need in order to retire and live well? How much money would you like to earn in order to help others who are in need? Write your financial dreams below.

YOUR FINANCIAL DREAMS

What things do you dream of having? What things would you like to buy? What things would you like to give away? Do you dream of owning a villa on the lake? A mansion in the hills? An airplane? A brand new suit? A Mercedes Benz? What things would you like to own? Write them in the spaces below.

YOUR MATERIAL DREAMS

What do you dream of experiencing? Where would you love to go? Would you like to vacation in Italy or Greece? Would you like to go skydiving? Whitewater rafting? Would you like to go bungee jumping? Would you like to bring in the New Year in Times Square? Visit the Vatican? Write your dreams below.

YOUR EXPERIENTIAL DREAMS

What dreams do you have for your relationships? Do you dream of having a happy, healthy marriage? Do you dream of having a great relationship with your parents? Do you want to repair a relationship with your siblings? With your co-workers? With your teachers? With your classmates? Write them below.

YOUR RELATIONAL DREAMS

What are your spiritual goals? Do you want to grow spiritually? Write down some of your spiritual goals below.

YOUR SPIRITUAL DREAMS

By writing down your dreams, you have moved one step closer to making your dreams a reality. You have gotten more clarity about what you really want out of life. You are no longer just hoping for something in general, but you are hoping for some things that are very specific. That specificity is key for your success. That focus is foundational.

To be sure, there is much more work to be done; but getting clear about your dreams is essential to every other step that we will discuss in the rest of the book. So congratulations! If you have made it this far in the book, then you are already further along than most people who buy books like this. I am so glad you are taking this journey seriously. Your next chapter in life is going to be all the better for it.

CHAPTER 5

YOUR BELIEFS

How do you achieve your dreams? I am convinced that where we are right now, and who we are right now, is the result of the steps, the actions, we have taken in our past; I believe that our steps, or our actions, grow out of the decisions that we have made; and, I am convinced, beyond a shadow of a doubt, that the decisions we make grow out of the beliefs that we have in our heads and hearts. Consequently, where we are, and who we are, right now, is ultimately the result of the beliefs in our heads and hearts that we have acted upon. Our beliefs govern our decisions, and our decisions determine our actions, and our actions determine our future. If you want to achieve anything in life, you have to make sure that you have the right beliefs in your head and heart to get you there.

Your beliefs are the foundation upon which your life rests. That's why I spent the whole last chapter laying the proper foundation. I want you to have the right beliefs in your head.

One of the most important beliefs you can have is the belief in yourself. One of the hardest things I've ever done is believe in myself, that I could achieve my dreams if I really gave my all.

If you're going to create the life of your dreams, you're going to have to develop a healthy self-confidence, which gives you the belief you need to accomplish anything meaningful. How you see yourself is foundational to everything you think, say, feel, and do. Your thoughts about yourself determine almost everything else in your life.

One of my favorite poems by Walter Wintle says:

If you think you are beaten, you are
If you think you dare not, you don't,
If you like to win, but you think you can't,
It is almost a certain, you won't.

If you think you'll lose, you've lost
For out of the world we find,
Success begins with a fellow's will
It's all in the state of mind.

If you think you are outclassed, you are
You've got to think high to rise,
You've got to be sure of yourself before
You can ever win the prize.

Life's battles don't always go
To the stronger or faster man,
But soon or late the one who wins
Is the man who thinks he can.

In order to achieve your dreams, you're going to have to believe that *they can* be achieved, and that *you can* achieve them.

You. Yes, YOU! The truth is, the man who thinks he can; and the man who thinks he can't, are both right. Your belief in your ability to make your dream a reality is an inescapable must for you. You have to believe that you are smart enough, strong enough, committed enough to make that dream or goal a reality.

Now, I'm not saying that you need to lie to yourself. Rather, I am saying that you need to eliminate any limiting beliefs you have in your head that may be causing you to miss out on great opportunities. Sometimes other people don't believe in you; sometimes other people will doubt you. But who cares? You don't need them to believe in you. Believe in yourself. Even if no one else believes in you, you have to believe in you.

Why is this so important? Because how you feel about yourself (your self-esteem) is directly related to how you see yourself (your self-image). How you feel determines what you do. In other words, how you see yourself determines how you feel about yourself, and how you feel about yourself largely determines your actions; your actions, when repeated, result in habits, and habits shape character. Character ultimately determines where you will end up.

Also, how much you like yourself is directly related to how well you relate to others. Only people with high self-images relate well with others on a consistent basis, which usually means you will have a better network of acquaintances and greater potential for opportunities. If you reverse that logic, you see that those without a healthy self-image will miss out on great friendships, business partners, and opportunities, which one needs to be truly successful.

Jesse Jackson, the civil rights leader, came up with a saying that he recited to remind people about how important they are. He would say a line or a phrase, and the audience would repeat it. It was a call and response kind of presentation, and it really spoke to the hearts of people:

I am somebody.
I may be poor, but I am somebody!
I may be on welfare, but I am somebody!
I may be uneducated, but I am somebody!
I may be young, but I am somebody!
I may be small, but I am somebody!
I may have made mistakes, but I am somebody!
My clothes are different, my face is different,
my hair is different, but I am somebody!
I am black, brown, or white, but I am precious in God's sight. I am somebody!
I speak a different language, but I must be respected, protected, never rejected. I must be, I'm God's child.

In the same way, although you may come from very humble beginnings, you must always remind yourself that you are somebody very special. You may have heard it said, "Just because you live in the ghetto doesn't mean that the ghetto has to live in you." The same truth applies to you. Just because you live a certain place, it doesn't mean that the negative, depressing, destructive conditions of that place have to live in you. You define your situation; your situation doesn't define you. You are greater than your situation. In fact, your worth is not tied to your circumstances, but rather to the fact that you are created with infinite beauty, worth, value, and purpose.

Believe in yourself. When no one else believes in you, you believe in you. Never allow someone else's negative opinion about you control your own opinion about yourself. You must control how you see yourself. When you make a mistake, it does not mean that you are a mistake. Just because you have failed at something, it does not mean that you are a failure. You are greater than your shortcomings. You are greater than your mistakes. You are greater than your circumstances.

You need to realize that, right now, in this moment, you have something inside you that can change your entire life. You have within you a power that is greater than your background, greater than your lack of education, greater than poverty, and greater than racism. It is the power to focus your mind and heart on your dreams and make those dreams a reality. You have been blessed with that power, but you have to put it to use. The dreams you have conceived in your head and heart must be married to your faith. You must believe. You must believe that you are enough. You must believe that you are able. You must believe that you are powerful. Only then, with that belief, can your dreams be achieved. So believe!

ASSIGNMENT #5
YOUR BELIEF IN YOURSELF

Write down a list of things you can say to yourself in the morning, and throughout the day to encourage yourself.

If you want to change your life, you need to change your mind. If you want to do anything great, you are going to have to take inventory of your beliefs; then, you are going to have to destroy and eliminate for good any beliefs that are working against you achieving your dreams.

Your mind can be your best friend, or your worst enemy. Your mind can set you up for success, or sabotage you for failure. Your mind, more than anything else, is the reason you are where you are right now in your life. What you have learned, from the day you were born until this very moment, together has landed you at this place in your life. So the question must be asked, "are you where you want to be? Are you who you want to be? Do you have what you want to have?" If your answer to those questions is a resounding no, then I submit to you that it is your beliefs that have been in your way. There are some things in your mind that have kept you from achieving the life that you want to have. There are some mental roadblocks, some psychological barriers, standing between where you are and where you want to be in your life.

A belief is a feeling of certainty about something. A belief is a feeling of confidence that something is true. It is a feeling that something in your head corresponds accurately to something that exists in the world. A belief is a feeling that something is true.

Where did your beliefs come from? How did you get them? Why do you still have them? I'm convinced that your beliefs grow out of your experiences. Things you have been through in your own life have caused you to adopt feelings of certainty about something. If something happens to you over and over again, eventually you start to form a pattern in your head that that something is true. For example, if you want to leave your home, then you need to open your front door and go outside. In order to open your front door, you have to turn the doorknob. Once you turn the knob, the door opens. You start to form a pattern in your head that turning doorknobs causes doors to open. That pattern causes you to form the belief that, "if turning this doorknob causes my door to open, then it might also work on other doors." So, whenever you see a door that is not your own, you believe that the pattern that worked on your own door will probably work on every other door. If you did not develop that pattern in your head, then you would never go outside. You would not know how to open other doors. You'd be stuck in your home forever!

Patterns can be good, and they can also be bad. I was speaking at a high school in Pennsylvania, and after I was done speaking, a young lady approached me. She was a little bit overweight, but nonetheless beautiful to me. I greeted her by giving her a hug, and said, "Hello, beautiful. How are you?"

The young lady shook her head, indicating that she didn't agree with what I just said. She said, "No."

Confused, I asked, "No, what? What do you mean?"

She replied, "Don't call me beautiful."

I smiled, and said, "but you are beautiful."

She shook her head again, and said, "No. No. No. ... No I'm not. I'm not beautiful."

My confusion turned to concern. "What do you mean? Sure, you're beautiful. Why don't you think so?"

She started crying, and said, "no one has ever called me that."

"You mean to tell me no one in your life has ever told you that you are beautiful, not even your parents?" I asked.

"No. You're the first person who has EVER called me that. I'm not beautiful. People have always called me fat, and ugly. No one has ever told me that they think I'm beautiful ..."

I spent the next thirty minutes counseling that young lady about her self-image.

Like that young lady, we may have some beliefs that are limiting us, holding us back, and robbing us of our potential. Your beliefs have a way of setting you up for success, or guaranteeing your failure. I have heard another person refer to those kinds of self-sabotaging beliefs as "stinkin' thinkin'."

One of the first things you need to do in this next chapter of your life is identify, and eliminate, any beliefs that are eliminating your prospects for success. So let's start with your dream. What is one of your dreams or goals? Just pick one of them.

The first thing you need to ask yourself is, "Is there any doubt in my head or heart that I can achieve that goal or dream?"

If you don't honestly think you can, then what you have identified is a limiting belief. If you think you are too poor to rise to great heights, then that's a limiting belief. If you believe that "people like me never make it," then you have identified one of your limiting beliefs.

Let's take a moment and list out some of the beliefs that are holding you back. I'll share some of my old limiting beliefs with you so you can understand what I'm talking about. Look at the table below.

LIMITING BELIEF	
Reading is boring!	
I am not smart enough to go to college.	
People like me don't deserve first-class treatment.	
I might fail if I try.	
Black people don't fly airplanes.	
All white people are racist.	
All men cheat on their wives.	
I'll never own my own home.	
I don't know how to be a good father.	
Our school systems are too broken to be fixed.	
People like me can't backpack through Europe.	

You've seen some of my old limiting beliefs. What are some of your own limiting beliefs?

LIMITING BELIEF	

HOW DO YOU GET RID OF YOUR LIMITING BELIEFS?

In order to eliminate these self-sabotaging beliefs that corrupt your thinking, it is not enough to wish them away. It is not enough to declare them to be gone. No, they are so deeply rooted in your psyche that it is going to take much more to rid them from your system.

You are going to have to link so much pain to that belief that your brain and body can no longer tolerate it. You have to link so much pain to that belief that, like a sickness, your body fights to rid it from its system.

In order to do that, you have to be very honest with yourself about what that belief has cost, is costing, and will cost you. I'll give you an example of how I did that with my belief that "I might fail if I try" to chase my dream of becoming self-employed.

The first thing I did was asked the question, "Manny, what have you missed out on because of your fear of failure?" I then answered that question as honestly as I could. I wrote something like, "If I wasn't afraid of failing, I would have tried harder in school. I missed out on making more friends. I missed out on possibly excelling in college football. I missed out on that job opening that could have led to more money and more responsibility. I missed out on buying my first home when I was 22 years old. I could have had many more properties by now had I taken more risks." I wrote for a while about the things my fear of failure has caused me to miss out on.

Next, I asked myself the question, "Manny, what are you missing out on right now because of your fear of failure?" I then answered that question again, by writing something like, "I am missing out on making more money. I am missing out on living free from the concern of others. I am robbing myself of the opportunity to do more with my potential. I am missing out on helping more people. I should be accomplishing more right now, but I am afraid of what others are going to say about me if I try to set myself apart from the majority of people. I am missing out on spending more time with my family. I am missing out …"

Finally, I asked myself, "Manny, if I keep living in fear of what others say about me, what will I miss out on this year, next year, in the next five years, ten years, twenty years, and so on?" My answer to that question became quite overwhelming. I said something like, "I will have to keep a job that is under-utilizing my potential. I will be more miserable because I'll be settling for less than my best. I'll probably be making the same amount of money. My wife won't be freed to pursue her own interests. My kids will not be able to experience the things that I would like them to experience. I won't be able to afford to give them the kind of life that I want them to have. My kids will probably learn to live in fear like their father, and grow up making choices out of fear and not faith. It will take me thirty years just to pay off this house. I won't be able to travel the world, or take vacations, or write books, or spend more time with my family and friends.

If I don't step out of my fears and into faith, how many people are going to give up? How many young people are going to commit suicide? How many people are going to make decisions that will ruin the rest of their lives? How many people will waste their lives if you don't get over this fear of what others think about you? …" I probably wrote two or three pages in my journal about what that belief would do to my life.

By doing that, I immediately began to grieve for myself. I felt the pain I would one day experience if something did not change. I envisioned myself growing old having never pressed through my fears. I saw myself old, and grumpy, and filled with regret. I saw myself as a man who had wasted his life. That vision of how my limiting belief could cause me to waste my life became so overwhelming that I became emotional.

Right there, in that moment, I realized that I had to change. I had to get through it, over, around it, destroy it, or replace it. I used my power to turn the page, and I decided that I was no longer going to be a "what-if" person. I was not going to be the person who grew old, and looked back over my life with regrets about things I never tried, complaining, "What if I would have tried harder in school? What if I would have asked that girl for her number? What if I would have tried to travel the world?" I read somewhere that most people who are on their death-beds, near the end of their lives, have more regrets about the things they didn't do than about the things they did. I decided that I didn't want to get to the end of my story and be sorry about all the life I wasted.

I confronted my limiting belief by replacing it. I decided to believe that it is much better to try and fail than to never try at all. I convinced myself that if I have everything to gain by trying, then by all means, I was going to try. Sure, I knew I would fail sometimes; but I also believed that anything worth doing, is worth doing poorly the first time.

I then asked myself, "how would my life change if I adopted this new belief?" I wrote something like, "I would achieve more. I would probably make more money, be more confident, and be less concerned about what other people think about me. I would learn a lot about myself as a person, and grow as a person, and become more of my best self. I would experience more adventure, and more excitement in my life. My kids would learn by watching me that life isn't about winning all the time; but about doing your best to win; and, even if you fail, you can get up, and try again. Failure is not a bad thing; it can actually be a powerful tool in motivating you to try even harder, and become even better the next time. If I took a risk on myself, then I would have more control over my schedule, and I would get to spend much more time with my family. I would get to travel the world, and I would be able to help a lot more people. I would be able to interrupt more suicides. I would be able to save some marriages. I would be able to help many more families create happy, healthy environments that are conducive for the success of everyone in the home, especially the children. I would make a lot more memories, and probably have a lot more fun …"

The more I wrote, the more excited I became. I could see myself enjoying my life so much more, and I could feel the joy and excitement that would come from living life like that.

Next, I found a quote from Theodore Roosevelt that undergirded my new belief. He said:

It is not the critic who counts; not the man who points out how the strong man stumbles, or where the doer of deeds could have done them better. The credit belongs to the man who is actually in the arena, whose face is marred by dust and sweat and blood; who strives valiantly; who errs, who comes short again and again, because there is no effort without error and shortcoming; but who does actually strive to do the deeds; who knows great enthusiasms, the great devotions; who spends himself in a worthy cause;

who at the best knows in the end the triumph of high achievement, and who at the worst, if he fails, at least fails while daring greatly, so that his place shall never be with those cold and timid souls who neither know victory nor defeat.

Now, when I sense fear trying to scare me out of doing something, I recite that quote, and I really ask myself, "why not? What's the worst that could happen to me if I try this?" If it won't kill me, or seriously hurt me, or hurt those I love, then I am more often than not going to give it a try. I tell myself, I would rather try, and fail, than not try at all. Life is too short to be crippled by that kind of belief. I'm going to try, and I might embarrass myself. I might even blow it. But who cares? At least I tried. At least I did my best.

My adoption of that new belief really changed the way I approached challenges and opportunities. It changed the way I looked at life. Now, I am not as reluctant to try something new, for I have learned that it will probably help me learn something new, and help me grow as a person.

That's what I did to eliminate just one of my limiting beliefs. Now it's your turn. Pick one of your limiting beliefs, and answer the questions in the table. Do not just go through the motions of answering the questions mindlessly. Also, because of the small size of these pages, I highly recommend you pull out your journal, or a piece of paper, and go through the assignment in your journal or on a separate piece of paper. Really put your head and heart into it, and something special can happen in your life. Look at the next page to see the table.

HOW TO ELIMINATE YOUR LIMITING BELIEFS

1. What is one of your limiting beliefs that is holding you back?

2. What have you missed out on in your past because of that belief? Write a paragraph.

3. What are you missing out on right now because of that belief? Write a paragraph.

4. What will you miss out on in your future if you continue holding on to that belief? Write a paragraph. Write until you see yourself growing old with that belief. Write until you feel the pain that the limiting belief will cause in your life. Write until you feel the pain that such a belief will cause you. Write until you feel how much that belief will cost you, if you do not eliminate it.

HOW TO ELIMINATE YOUR LIMITING BELIEFS

5. What is a more empowering belief that you can replace that old belief with? What belief would better position you to reach your goals, achieve your dreams?

6. How would my life change if I adopted this new belief? Write a paragraph about how this new belief could really change how you think, how you feel, and how you behave. Write until you feel the pleasure and joy that the new belief can create for you.

7. What are some quotes from music, poetry, books, or television that reinforce your new, empowering belief? Write them down here.

Hopefully, you did not just go through the motions above, but you really put your heart into that above assignment. If you put your heart into, I believe that something in your head and heart began to change.

I did that exercise for many of the beliefs that were holding me back. Below is my list of limiting beliefs again, and a list of the empowering beliefs with which I replaced them.

LIMITING BELIEF	EMPOWERING BELIEF
Reading is boring!	Books are conversations waiting to be picked up.
I am not smart enough to go to college.	I can learn anything if I apply myself.
People like me don't deserve first-class treatment.	I deserve to be treated as well as anyone else.
I might fail if I try.	It is better to try and fail than never try at all.
Black people don't fly airplanes.	I'll become the first African-American I know to become a pilot.
All white people are racist.	Many white people are as loving and kind as anyone else.
All men cheat on their wives.	I can and will stay faithful.
I'll never own my own home.	I can become a successful real estate investor.
I don't know how to be a good father.	I can become the father I never had.
Our school systems are too broken to be fixed.	I can do my best to help as many people in the school system as possible.
People like me can't backpack through Europe.	I can go anywhere I want to go if I work hard, plan, and save my money.

My limiting beliefs held me back for years. They kept me from trying, and they robbed me of precious time and many opportunities. But I got to a place in my life when I got tired of life passing me by. I grew frustrated by my lack of progress as a person. I got angry with myself for allowing myself to become such a passive recipient of the garbage that life had heaped upon me.

You can do the same thing, but you have to start by addressing the software in your head, the data in your brain, that might be limiting you. That's where your change will take place. Your decisions, actions, and destiny, all depend upon the quality of your beliefs.

ASSIGNMENT #6
ELIMINATE YOUR BARRIERS

As we bring this chapter to a close, I need to give you another assignment. I want you to identify your limiting, disempowering beliefs, and work to eliminate them, one by one. That's what I did in my own life; and that's what you are going to have to do in your own life, in order to create the life of your dreams.

CHAPTER 7
YOUR ATTITUDE

I recently earned my instrument rating in my airplane and the training was at times very intense. We were flying at 6,500 feet above the ground when my flight instructor made me close my eyes and put my chin on my chest. I was already wearing a view-limiting device that prevented me from seeing outside, so when he made me close my eyes, and put my head down, it made things quite interesting.

He then told me to fly the airplane based on how I felt. If I felt I was turning, to straighten myself out. If I felt I was climbing or descending, to correct it, based on my feelings only. While I was flying with my eyes closed, I started feeling all disoriented. I felt like I was turning to the right, so I adjusted the airplanes yoke (steering wheel) to the left. When I thought I was climbing, I pushed my yoke forward to stop the climb and level out. After about four minutes of flying with my eyes closed, something felt really wrong. My flight instructor then told me to open my eyes.

My attitude indicator, or artificial horizon, which is a mechanical substitute for the natural horizon, was turned completely sideways, indicating a steep bank and rapid descent. It is the only instrument in the plane that gives you an immediate and direct indication of the airplane's pitch and bank attitude. The attitude indicator lets you know if your plane is climbing or descending. It lets you know if you are going up or down. It also lets you know if you are banking left or right. When I opened my eyes, I quickly scanned my instrument panel, and focused on the attitude indicator, and saw my plane was banked at a 45-degree angle to the right, we were losing over 2,500 feet per minute, and we were spiraling toward the ground. I had entered into the beginning phase of a graveyard spiral, the very thing that killed John F. Kennedy Jr.! I also noticed out of the corner of my view-limiting device that we were inside of a cloud!

I eventually came out of the cloud, and looked up only to see the earth was getting bigger and bigger in my windshield! If I didn't do something soon, we were going to become a ball of fire. So I reduced the power to slow our descent, I leveled the wings to break the spiral, and I slowly pulled back on the yoke while watching my attitude indicator. Once the little, artificial plane's wings on the attitude indicator were level with the attitude indicator's artificial horizon, I knew that I had stopped our descent, and returned the plane to straight and level flight. I then increased my power, and pulled back on the yoke so I could climb back up to six-thousand, five-hundred feet.

My attitude indicator allowed me to see that I was in a steep-bank, and that I was dropping like a boulder out of the sky. It also let me know when I was climbing back up to my desired altitude. When the wings on the attitude indicator are above the artificial horizon, then my plane climbs; if the wings are below the artificial horizon of the attitude indicator, then the plane descends. In an airplane, the attitude indicator determines your altitude. It determines if you are going up, or if you are going down.

In the same way, your attitude in life determines your altitude. If your life seems to be spiraling out of control, then you might need to take a careful look at your attitude. If you feel like you can't get above the clouds in your life, then you might want to take a look at your attitude.

I think it was John Maxwell who says that your attitude is an inward feeling expressed by outward behavior. If you tend to focus on the negatives in every situation, then your life is going to be filled with negativity. If you think everyone is trying to hurt you, or take advantage of you, or take your place, then you might have an attitude problem. If you are constantly thinking that everything is about you, then you might have an attitude problem. If you cannot admit that you are wrong, then you definitely have an attitude problem. If you can't forgive people who have done you wrong, you might have an attitude problem. If you are always comparing yourself to others, and you find yourself constantly trying to point out their flaws, then you have an attitude problem. If you always want the credit, but never take the blame, then you have an attitude problem. If you are always criticizing other people, then you have an attitude problem. If you don't address that attitude problem, then soon enough, you are going to find your life spiraling out of control, and you will find yourself heading straight toward the ground. If, however, you keep looking up, focusing on the positive things in life, you will climb, and begin rising above the clouds of misery and mediocrity. Your attitude determines your altitude.

Your attitude also determines your access. In life, your attitude determines whether or not you get access to people and positions of influence. People of power and influence prefer to have people around them who have positive attitudes. If you are known as someone who is ever negative, why would anyone want to be in your presence?

One of the most important things you can do to make sure the next chapters of your life are great is keep a positive mental attitude. I have met so many people in my life who have seen everything through the lens of negativity. They always look for the worst in other people, they look for the worst in every situation.

Not you, though. I want you to work on developing a healthy, positive attitude. Sure, having a positive attitude alone will not fix all your problems, or make everything better; but having positive mental attitude enables you to do everything better than a negative mental attitude ever will. Having a positive mental attitude will help you lose weight better than a bad attitude. A positive attitude will help you perform better in school than a bad one; it will help you on your job better than a bad one; it will help you with your relationships more than a bad one; it will help you make more money than a bad one. Having a good attitude is so much more useful for you than a negative one is.

How then can one improve his or her attitude? First, ask yourself how your attitude might be helping or hurting you. How has your attitude affected your health? How is your attitude affecting your grades, your job, your money, your relationships, your spirit? Is your attitude lifting you up, or pulling you down? Write down areas where your attitude needs to change. Write down the consequences of not changing it; write down the rewards for changing it.

Managing your vocabulary is another way you can improve your attitude. Change your vocabulary from disempowering statements to empowering statements.

Instead of saying, "I can't," say "I can."

Change "I have to" to "I choose to."

Change "they made me feel" to "I allowed them to make me feel."

Change "I doubt" to "I believe and expect."

Change "it's not possible" to "it is possible."

Change "I don't have time" to "I will make time."

Change "I'm ugly" to "I'm beautiful."

Change "I'm worthless" to "I'm invaluable."

Change "life is a struggle" to "life is an adventure."

Change "life is misery" to "life is an opportunity."

Change "I'm not smart enough" to "I can learn anything I set my mind to."

There might be some other things you have in your vocabulary that you need to change. I highly recommend you start changing those things today. Change the way you talk to yourself. Change the way you think about yourself. Change the way you think about others. You have much more power than you realize. You can make even the most difficult situations better with the right attitude.

There was a woman I greatly admired named Pam Howard.

She had cancer, and was terminally ill. Yet, when I went to visit her, she was always so upbeat and kind. She was always encouraging. Her attitude deeply affected me. I used to go over there to encourage her, but she was the one who encouraged me. I am pretty sure I walked away from my times with her more encouraged than she was. She was so kind, and so loving.

Her positive attitude, despite her sickness, was really special. It was rooted in her faith that all things would somehow work together for a greater good. I was with her the night she passed away. Pam impacted so many people in her life with her positive attitude, rooted in her strong faith and amazing love, that they had to have her funeral at a huge arena-like venue. There was standing room only. It was one of the most beautiful funerals I have ever seen. Pam, despite having cancer, did not allow that sickness to steal her joy. Her attitude didn't cure her of cancer, but it sure changed a lot of lives.

My friend, your attitude determines your altitude, your access, and your influence. Choose to see things in the most positive light possible; it has the power to make your life, and the world, so much better.

When I was younger, we did not have a lot of money. My mom

ASSIGNMENT #7
ATTITUDE ASSESSMENT

How's your attitude? What can you do to improve it?

CHAPTER 8
YOUR ENVIRONMENT

When I was younger, we did not have a lot of money. My mom used to take me and my brothers to Goodwill or to Payless ShoeSource to buy our shoes. And you know, as a kid, when you put on a new pair of shoes, you thought you could run really fast. I used to have shoes that didn't have a name brand or anything like that. But when you're little, you don't really know that you're poor until you get around other people who aren't poor. Well, my brothers stopped going with us to Payless, and it wasn't until I got to middle school that I understood why they stopped getting their shoes from Payless.

When I got to middle school, I started getting clowned for my outfits and shoes. Other kids had Jordans, and Nikes, and Reeboks, and Adidas, but I had on Payless shoes. I went home, and begged my mom to buy me some Nikes too. My mom has never really cared about things like that so she took me to Payless, and convinced me to buy some shoes that looked like Nikes. Even though I was reluctant to buy the shoes, she convinced me that she could make them look just like Nikes. We got home, and my mom took out a big black magic marker and drew a Nike swoosh on the side of each shoe.

But because I didn't really know anything about Nikes, I thought she had done a good job. Well, when I got to school the next day, one of my classmates stopped me, kneeled down, looking at my shoes, and said, "ah, no way!" He then called a bunch of people over, and said, "look, this fool drew the swoosh on his shoes!" And they fell out laughing. I didn't know how they could tell that mine was fake until I compared my swoosh with theirs. Mine was backwards! I think I ditched school, went home, and threw my shoes in the dumpster!

I look back at that, and many other experiences in my life, and I realize how silly I was. I look back at those memories and just laugh. I wanted those shoes so badly. I wanted my classmates to think I was as cool as they were. I wanted the girls to be impressed by my shoes. I wanted to fit in. I didn't want to be different. I didn't want to be unique. I didn't want to be me. I wanted to be just like everyone else.

Now that I'm much older, I realize that not much has changed. The desire to be popular, esteemed, and respected shows up in how so many young people are behaving at school. Since the "cool" kids, the "in" group, make fun of people for excelling academically, calling them "square" for getting good grades, or think you're acting "white" for taking school seriously, you then alter your behavior so that they won't make fun of you anymore. So they won't think you're different.

I also see this desire to be accepted showing up in how people behave around members of the opposite sex. Because certain behaviors get the attention of certain guys, some girls begin offering the same services as those other girls, just so a guy can pay attention to them.

Furthermore, I see this desire to be accepted showing up among young men who are glorifying "thug" life. They are smoking weed, often disrespectful to authority, and are not taking school seriously. Some of them are carrying guns. Despite those things, many young ladies are drooling over them. As a result, other guys who would like to attract the attention of those girls are trying to dress like they are hard. They feel as though they need to act hard, smoke weed, and talk back to teachers or administrators.

This desire to be popular, esteemed, and respected causes people to start cussing because they think it makes them sound grown. It pushes people to start smoking cigarettes because they think it makes them look mature. It pushes them to twerk, or drop it like it's hot, or whatever the latest dance is, just so guys will be attracted to them.

This desire to fit in, to be like everyone else, still influences much of our behavior today. Kanye West, the Chicago lyricist acknowledges this when he says:

> We buy our way out of jail, but we can't buy freedom
> We'll buy a lot of clothes when we don't really need em
> Things we buy to cover up what's inside
> Cause they make us hate ourself and love they wealth
> That's why shortys hollering "where the ballas' at?"
> Drug dealer buy Jordans, crackheads buy crack
> And a white man get paid off of all of that
> But I ain't even gonna act holier than thou
> Cause *&#! it, I went to Jacob with 25 thou
> Before I had a house and I'd do it again

Cause I wanna be on 106 and Park pushing a Benz
I wanna act ballerific like it's all terrific
I got a couple past due bills, I won't get specific
I got a problem with spending before I get it
We all self conscious I'm just the first to admit it.

Kanye West admits that many people have been "made to hate" themselves and to love material things, so that they can impress others. But even after acknowledging what is being done to us, he says, unashamedly, that he would buy those things again. Many of us, like Kanye West himself admits, have bought into the need to be admired, respected, to fit in. Many of us are self conscious. We wonder what people think about us; we wonder whether they think we are attractive; we wonder whether they think we are smart enough; we wonder whether we are good enough.

All of this, I am convinced, is rooted in our desire to be accepted. All of us want to be loved. All of want someone to tell us that they accept us; all of us want to be esteemed and respected; all of us have in us a thirst for affirmation; we want someone else to say that we belong; that we fit in.

To find that affirmation, to find that love, to find that acceptance, people often do things that compromise who they are. They tell small lies to cover someone's mistake; they cheat so they can look smart; they sleep with people to feel loved; they smoke weed to be fit in; they get drunk to numb the pain. Those behaviors eventually lead people into a deeper, darker, self-destructive pit. But where does this desire come from?

Many of us don't realize that much of what we do has been influenced by a man named Edward Bernays, who became the father of the public relations industry in the 20s. He said, "It is now possible to control and regiment the masses according to our will without their knowing it." He said, "through radio, television, newspapers, magazines, and other media, we can now regiment people's minds like the military regiments their bodies." In other words, we can exercise "thought control."

The idea was that in a country in which the government can't control the people by force, it had better control what people think. Techniques were designed to "control" people's minds. So even though schools ought to provide people with techniques of mental self-defense, many democratic theorists have understood for 60 or 70 years that if you can't control people's behavior by force, then you have to control how they think. Because if you can control how they think, then you can control what they say, and what they do.

Democratic theorists began to see schools as a means to indoctrinate the young. "They are institutions for indoctrination, for imposing obedience, for blocking the possibility of independent thought, and they play an institutional role in a system of control" of the masses.

Furthermore, in his book, *The Media Monopoly*, Ben Badgikian says that by the end of the late 90s, just ten companies controlled most of the U.S. media landscape- down from 50 in 1983. "They control music, movies, magazines, television, video games, and the internet." Chuck D, of Public Enemy, puts it like this: "five companies own all major retail; there are four major record labels; there are three who own all the radio stations; there are two major television networks who own all the others; and there is really just one video outlet." The point I'm making is that only about 10 companies control what we hear, watch, read, and wear. The leaders of these companies determine which shows get aired, what type of music gets played, what type of clothes gets marketed. The leaders of these companies are literally brainwashing the country.

That's why it is so important for you to watch what you expose yourself to. Your brain is constantly being pitched beliefs that can seriously affect your thoughts, feelings, and actions. If you are not careful, the media can convince you to try to be someone you are not. It can influence you to become an imitation of someone else.

Don't conform yourself, or change your own behavior to be like other people. Don't allow someone else to change you; don't allow that environment to change you into being like other people in it. If you are not careful, the people you hang around can change you. If you are not careful, the environments that you are in most often can change you. Just because other people cuss, you don't have to cuss; just because other people smoke, you don't smoke; just because other girls are giving it up, you don't have to give it up; just because other guys want to act like they're hard, you don't act like that; just because they have cheated their way to that corner office, you don't cheat to get to the corner office; just because they are impatient with you, you don't get impatient with them; just because they think you're a square for getting good grades, you don't pay them any attention. Because you are not like them, you are not designed to be like them, and in fact, you are not supposed to be like them.

You see it happen to people all the time. People you once thought were solid start hanging with a group and they begin to adopt the same mentality as the other people in the group. Even if they don't agree with something, because they are new, or young, or inexperienced, or lack self-confidence, they keep quiet, and just accept wrong as though it is right. They let their environment change them.

Not you. Be very careful about what you expose yourself to. Be very careful about who you spend your time with. Be very careful about the environments you frequent, because those environments can plant a belief in your head and heart that can sabotage your success. Guard your thoughts. Guard your beliefs. Guard what you let get into your head and heart. Take every thought captive, and weigh whether it will limit you or empower you.

ASSIGNMENT #8
PICK YOUR PLACE

How would you describe your environment? Is it healthy or unhealthy? Encouraging or discouraging? Does it bring out the good in you, or the bad? Does it inspire you to grow, or make you want to give up? Be honest with yourself. Then list out a few healthy places you will spend most of your time from this day forward.

CHAPTER 9

YOUR ROADMAP

I was once driving my family from Denver, Colorado, to Sterling, a small, rural town in the northeast corner of the state. It was my first time driving to Sterling. Because I had ridden to Sterling as a passenger many times before the trip, I didn't really think the drive would be all that hard. We had been on the road for about an hour when everyone else in the car had fallen asleep. Since I am an adventurous person, I found myself appreciating the beauty of the scenery and the tranquility of the ride. After a while, I was running low on gas, so I pulled over, filled up the gas tank, and went inside the mini-mart to grab some snacks. While paying for my items at the counter, I let the cashier know I was driving from Denver, and asked him how much longer I had to drive before I got to Sterling. Looking at me in disbelief, he blurted out, "Sir, you're in Nebraska!"

I thought I could make it from Denver to Sterling on my gut feelings, so I never bothered to get a map, and didn't stop and ask for directions. As a result, I ended up in a place that did not intend to be.

If you want to turn the page, and turn your dreams into reality, you need to know that having a dream is not enough. A dream without a plan is just wishful thinking. You need a "roadmap"—a plan—to get you from where you are to where you want to be, so that you can maximize the use of your time, energy, and resources.

As I begin this chapter on planning, let me make this clear: If you have a dream, you don't have to have all the answers to make that dream a reality. What you need is a commitment to achieve that dream, no matter what. No matter what people say about you. No matter what your family has said about you. No matter what the media says about you. No matter what your mistakes says about you. No matter what your circumstances say about you. No matter what your bank account says about you. I'm convinced that if you have a big enough commitment, your "How?" will reveal itself. When your "Why?" or your "Where?" is big enough, your "How?"—your plan—will find its way to you.

Having said that, I still believe that planning can help you in a lot of ways. Planning helps you get more specific about exactly where you want to go, who you would like to be, what you would like to achieve.

Now there are people who believe that planning is pointless. They sometimes say things like, "If you want to make God laugh, then tell him your plans." What they're saying, in essence, is that even the best-laid plans never really work. As a result, they live their lives in the spur of the moment. They just kind of go-with-the-flow, and hope things work out.

While I too believe in living spontaneously, and living in the moment (up to a point), I also believe in planning. For example, when I am on vacation, I don't really like to have an agenda. I like to rest, and just see what happens. We might go for a walk, or go swimming, or hang out on a beach, or enjoy a museum. Then, while enjoying the moment, something might pop up that seems interesting or fun to do. So we might go indoor skydiving at the last minute, or rolling down a hill, or have a snowball fight. Things like that just happen.

However, even my best family vacations have involved some planning. We planned where we wanted to go, and figured out how much we would have to budget for the vacation. We planned when we were going to go. We planned how we were going to get there, and where we were going to stay. On our family vacations, my wife and I usually have a list of things that we might want to do, and then once we are at our destination, we decide daily whether or not we are going to try anything that's on our list.

I believe there is a middle ground between planning everything out and living in the moment. I believe it is helpful to have a desired goal or dream in mind, and then to have a tentative plan to help you get to that destination. From my experience, no plan has ever worked out perfectly; but, my plans, once executed, usually get me closer to the place I intended to go. That middle ground allows you to have a sense of where you want to go, and it allows you some flexibility on your journey to get there.

Why is planning so important? Because most people have a dream; few people actually have a map to get there. In fact, most people never take their dreams out of their minds and hearts, and break it down into practical, realistic, written goals. That's called a plan, and that's what you need. Your plan is your map that will help get you to, or near, your desired destination.

Your plan, or "roadmap," lets you know where to turn left, when to turn right, and how long you are supposed to stay on that road, and when you are supposed to exit.

How do you develop a plan? That's what this chapter is all about.

DETERMINE WHERE YOU ARE

If you want to drive from your house to Disney World in Florida, you would need a map to get you from your current address to 3111 World Dr., Lake Buena Vista, FL. Disney World represents your dream; your home represents your current situation, your reality. To achieve your dreams, you drive from your home (your current reality) to Florida (your dream).

Before you get on the freeway, you need to make sure you have enough gas in the car, enough snacks to eat, money and credit cards, enough clothes for the journey, some books or reading materials, some DVDs, an iPod, and anything else you might want or need. Before you jump in the car and head for Florida, you need to make sure you have what you need for the journey.

In the same way, when it comes to your dreams, before you just begin rushing to make your dream a reality, you want to take an honest, careful, clear-headed look at yourself to make sure you have what you need for the journey. For example, if you want to become a lawyer, but you are still in middle or high school, then the first thing you need to do is look at your grades. How are your grades? More specifically, how well do you read and write? Can you write an essay that has a clear thesis, a body that flows, has supporting arguments, illustrations, transitions, and conclusions?

Also, do you have a hard time making it to appointments on time? Where are you mentally, emotionally, academically, professionally, and physically? How is your credit? How much debt do you have? What are your insecurities? What are your strengths? How is your relationship with your father and mother? Were you abused as a child, or are there any mental or emotional scars that you have for which you need to see a counselor? Are you on academic probation, or are you on the honor roll? Are you a member of any pre-law clubs, or do you know anyone who is a lawyer or judge?

When you own a business that sells products like books, shirts, pants, or video games, you have to take inventory. Taking inventory is required for tax and business purposes, and it lets you know exactly how many goods you have in your building at any given moment. You go through each of the items in your storage room, and you look carefully at what you have, and then you figure out what you need in order to make sure you have enough items in stock for your customers.

In the same way, if you want to be successful, you have to go into the storage room of your own heart and mind and take inventory. You have to look up and down the aisles, and check how much passion you have in your reserve. How much character do you have? Are you a responsible person? Are you really committed to making it to your destination?

"FORGET" YOUR PAST

Some time ago, my wife, Alice, and I ran in a 10k race. While I was running in that race, I remember running one mile, and feeling a little winded. I made it to the second-mile mark, and

I was even more tired. When I made it past the third, and then to the fourth mile, I was literally struggling to keep my legs moving. And something began to happen. I began to think about all of the people I had passed up, all of the miles I had already run, and I began to feel good about myself. I thought about the fact that I had made it 4 miles, a feat that most people could not face. Even though I had about 2 more miles to go, I began to lose motivation. Why? The more I began to think about what I had already accomplished, the less motivated I became to keep moving forward.

In your own race to your dreams, are there any things in your past that are causing you to become complacent? Is there anything in your past that is causing you to be stagnant? Are there any accomplishments, mistakes, awards, or accolades that are limiting your potential? Do you come from a pretty good family? Did you attend some of the finest schools? Maybe you live in an exclusive neighborhood, or live in a very nice house. May I submit to you that you need to stop letting those things of your past negatively influence your present? Why? Because the more you find gratification and satisfaction in your past accomplishments, the less motivated you will be to press forward to newer, and dare I say, greater things.

That's what the word "forget" means. After listing out several of his own accomplishments, one of my role models once said, "This one thing I do, forgetting what lies behind." To "forget" does not mean that we are to force ourselves to have some kind of amnesia or senility about things in our past. While there are some people who seem to have the gift of selective memory, that's not what it really means to "forget." To "forget" means to refuse to let things that happened to you in the past prevent you from living abundantly in the present.

Also, to "forget" is not just a one-time deal. Rather, it is something that you have to keep doing over and over again, because there are several things that happened to you in your past, good and bad, that keep being replayed in your brain, stifling your possibilities, and keeping you from being better than you were yesterday.

What do you need to keep "forgetting" about in your own past? What memory, experience, triumph, or tragedy do you need to release? Your history was merely preparation for something greater. Don't live in it, learn from it, and move on.

ASSIGNMENT #9
WRITE OUT YOUR ROADMAP TO SUCCESS

After you have dreamed, gotten clear-headed about your current situation, and "forgotten" about some of your failures and accomplishments, you need to write down your plan in your journal. Keep in mind that your plans will probably change as you go, but it is better to have a written plan than to have no plan at all. At least with the written plan, you can learn about what worked and didn't work, and try something else. Without a plan, you are just shooting from the hip without any forethought or deliberation.

What should you write down in your plan?

#1. Write down your dreams.

We've already covered dreams in chapter 4, so I'll just post my list of dreams here as a reminder.

DREAM
I dream of myself traveling, speaking to people around the world, inspiring and equipping others to overcome their obstacles and achieve their dreams.
I dream of myself being a faithful, loyal husband to my wife.
I dream of being a loving father to my children.
I dream of being healthy in every area of my life: mentally, emotionally, spiritually, physically, and financially.
I dream of learning to fly airplanes.
I dream of owning my own home.
I dream of being financially free.

#2. Set Goals

Just pick one of your dreams for now; you can do this again for your other dreams. But for now, just focus on your biggest dream. How many steps do you need to take in order to make that dream or vision a reality? A goal is a step that brings you closer to your dreams. I read somewhere that your goals should be SMART: Specific, Measurable, Attainable, Realistic, and Timely. It is important for your goals to be specific and measurable so that you can be clear about whether you have reached them. Now, keep in mind what I said before: you don't have to have all the answers; you just need a commitment to achieve that dream, no matter what. With that said, it is good to have a general idea about when you would like to achieve a specific goal or dream.

You need your goals to be attainable and realistic, which means that it is actually possible for you to achieve them. What is realistic to you may not be realistic for other people. So make sure you are being honest with yourself about the attainability of your goals. I don't believe in knocking people's dreams, but I do believe that there are some things that are going to be harder to achieve for some people. For example, I could dream of going to the NBA all I want, but at this point in my life, I'm barely 5'10", I've never really been good at basketball, and I've never played on a basketball team. It is unlikely that I will ever have a shot at making anyone's basketball team. I have learned that sometimes even your best is not good enough.

My point? Ask yourself, "is this dream really something that I believe I can achieve?" If so, then go for it. My point here is just to encourage you to be very honest about your own abilities and talents. I don't want you to set yourself up for failure or extreme disappointment.

You also want your dreams to be timely, meaning they need to have a date next to them so that you can have a deadline to shoot for. In the chart below, it is important for your dreams and goals to have deadlines, otherwise, they end up being wishful thinking.

I've chosen doctor as a dream to illustrate what I'm talking about. If you dream of being a doctor, then your goals would include some of the things listed on the following table:

DREAM/VISION: I dream of myself being a doctor who saves lives.		
ORDER OF PRIORITY	GOAL	DEADLINE: (date you plan to reach this goal)
	Graduate from college.	
	Work at the best hospital in the world.	
	Start my own medical practice.	
	Graduate from high school.	
	Graduate from medical school.	
	Complete my residency requirements.	

Now think of one of your dreams/visions, and then figure out how many goals/steps you will need to take to make it to that dream. List out your own goals in the "GOAL" column on the next page.

DREAM/VISION: I dream of myself (write your dream here) _____		
ORDER OF PRIORITY	**GOAL**	**DEADLINE:** (date you plan to reach this goal)

In my example, you will notice that my goals are out of order. If I wanted to be a doctor, I would first have to graduate from high school before I could graduate from college. So I would put a number "1" next to "graduate from high school." Then, my next goal would be to graduate from college. So, I would put a number "2" next to "graduate from college." Look at my example below.

DREAM/VISION: I dream of myself being a doctor who saves lives.		
ORDER OF PRIORITY	GOAL	DEADLINE: (date you plan to reach this goal)
2	Graduate from college.	
5	Work at the best hospital in the world.	
6	Start my own medical practice.	
1	Graduate from high school.	
3	Graduate from medical school.	
4	Complete my residency requirements.	

Now you do the same thing with your own goals. Place them in order. Which one must you reach first, second, third, and so on, in order to achieve your dream? Now go back to your list of GOALS, and prioritize your own goals in the column marked "ORDER of PRIORITY." Do that now.

Now that you have listed out your goals, and now that you have placed them in order of priority, you must put a date next to each of your goals. If I wanted to be a doctor, I would go to my goal marked with the number 1, and I would need to figure out how long it will take for me to reach that goal. Write that in the column marked "DEADLINE: DATE WHEN YOU PLAN TO REACH THIS GOAL" See my example:

DREAM/VISION: I dream of myself being a doctor who saves lives.		
ORDER OF PRIORITY	GOAL	DEADLINE: (date you plan to reach this goal)
2	Graduate from college.	Summer 2015
5	Work at the best hospital in the world.	Summer 2019
6	Start my own medical practice.	Summer 2023
1	Graduate from high school.	Summer 2026
3	Graduate from medical school.	August 2026
4	Complete my residency requirements.	January 1, 2030

Now go back to your list of GOALS, and figure out the deadlines for each of your own goals. Find a calendar online, and set your own deadlines. If you are not sure exactly when you plan to have reached your goal, try to take a realistic guess at when you plan to reach that goal. Be sure that you give yourself enough time to complete each goal. Be realistic with yourself. Do that now.

#3: Set Your Objectives

Great job! You have written your dream/s down on paper. You have written the goals you need to achieve in order to get you from where you are now to your dreams. You have also listed out deadlines of when you plan to reach your goals. Now it's time for you to get even more specific.

What specific things will you have to do to reach your first goal? If I wanted to become a doctor, my first goal would be to graduate from high school. In order to graduate from high school there are certain classes that I have to take. Those are objectives. See my example:

GOAL: Graduate from High School
Objective: I need to successfully complete 4 units of English (You could really list each class as one separate objective, since each one requires you to complete different assignments. For example Grammar, composition, literature, and poetry are different English classes that you could take).
Objective: I need to successfully complete 3 units of Mathematics (Algebra I, Algebra II, Geometry…)
Objective: I need to successfully complete 3 units of Laboratory Science (Biology, Chemistry, Physics)
Objective: I need to successfully complete 3 units of History and Citizenship Skills (US History, Oklahoma History, US Government, Geography, Econ…)
Objective: I need to successfully complete 2 units of the Same Foreign Language: (Spanish, French, German)
Objective: need to successfully complete 1 unit of Fine arts: (Drama, music, art…)

You may have noticed that every goal must have some objectives. Just like goals move you one step closer to your dreams, objectives move you one step closer to reaching your goals.

Now you try. Write your top goal in the space below marked "GOAL." What objectives must you achieve in order to reach your first goal? Write your objectives in the below spaces. Also, when (due date) do you plan on achieving each objective? Write that date in the "DEADLINE" column.

GOAL:	
OBJECTIVE	**DEADLINE**

#4: Determine Your Action Steps

You are almost done! Now that you have your dreams, goals, and objectives, there is just one more step in the planning phases that you must complete. You must now come up with some action steps for each objective. Just like goals get you closer to your dreams, and like objectives get you closer to your goals, action steps get you closer to fulfilling your objectives. What is an action step? *An action step is exactly what you must do in order to reach your objective.* This is the most specific part of your planning process.

Let me show you how it works. If I want to be a doctor, then I would first need to graduate from high school. In order to graduate from high school, I would need to accomplish my objectives (or pass all my classes). One of my objectives is to successfully complete 4 units (or classes) of English (technically, that's four different objectives; one for each class/unit). How do I do that? That's where the action step comes in. The action step tells me exactly what I must do to complete each English class. Let's take a look at my example on the next page:

GOAL: Graduate from High School	
OBJECTIVE: Successfully complete 11th grade English.	
ACTION STRATEGY	**DEADLINE**
Visit guidance counselor to request the English class that I want.	9/1/15
Attend class on the first day of school to get my syllabus from my English teacher.	9/15/15
Check-out books on the syllabus from the library.	9/15/15
List all my assignments and put deadlines next to them.	9/16/15
Read *Freedom Writers Diary*	10/1/15
Write rough draft of reflection paper on *Freedom Writers Diary*.	10/3/15
Edit rough draft of reflection paper.	10/7/15
Write final draft of reflection paper.	10/15/15
Turn in final draft of reflection paper on *Freedom Writers Diary*.	10/17/15

Notice that every one of your goals has more than one objective. The same thing can be said about objectives, because every objective will have several action steps. It's not that complicated. Just remember, *"Dreams need goals, goals need objectives, and objectives need action steps."*

It's your turn now. List out your top goal in the GOAL box. Then write your top objective in the OBJECTIVE box. Next, write down your ACTION STRATEGIES. If you are not sure exactly when your assignments are due, try to guess at the deadlines for now:

GOAL: Graduate from High School	
OBJECTIVE: Successfully complete 11th grade English.	
ACTION STRATEGY	DEADLINE

Congratulations! You finished your roadmap to success for one of your dreams. What you just did for one of your dreams and goals, you can now do for every one of your dreams and goals. Start with your dream/vision, and then write your roadmap to get you from where you are to where you want to be (goals, objectives, and action steps). Take your next goal, and do the same thing for that goal. Just repeat the process for every goal, and you will be one step closer to turning your dreams into reality.

#5: Meditate on Your Plan

Now that you have your plan, your roadmap written down on paper, it is important that you let it become your internal GPS, your internal guide that lets you know when to turn left or right. A GPS tells you how much farther you have to drive before you need to turn. It beeps when you are getting close to your turn or destination. And if you miss a turn, it tells you what you need to do in order to get back on track.

That GPS needs to be internalized by you. It needs to dominate your mind. When you wake up in the morning, one of the first things you need to do is look at your plan.

For example, when I was a little boy, we used to live in Colorado. Every now and then, my brothers and I used to visit farms to see the animals. I often would go hang out by the cows. And sometimes I would watch the cows eat. I noticed that cows seemed like they were always chewing. They just look at you, chew, and "moo" while chewing. I learned that cattle make jaw movements (or chew) about 40-60,000 times per day! That's because when they eat, they chew the grass or hay, they swallow it, and because they are ruminants, which means they have a digestive system that allows them to regurgitate their food, they regurgitate their meals, and chew on it some more (that's really gross, by the way!). They turn the cud over in their mouths and then swallow it; they then eat some more, turn it over in their mouths, swallow it, regurgitate it, turn it over in their mouths, and they swallow it again (I call that "doing way too much!"). That's where the phrase, "chewing one's cud" comes from, and it means, figuratively, to meditate or ponder. It means to chew on something in your mind and heart, turning it over again and again.

When it comes to your ROADMAP to YOUR DREAMS, you need to eat, chew, swallow, regurgitate, turn over, and swallow your dream and plan over again and again. In other words, you need to internalize that plan, keep it on your mind, and discuss it with others whom you can trust. That plan needs to be on your mind, in your heart, and on your agenda every day. When you wake up in the morning, your next major goal needs to be on your mind.

I know this sounds like a lot of information. It is. Success isn't going to come easy. Everyone has a dream, but only a few people have a plan. You have just been given tools to write down your plan, and create your ROADMAP to achieve your dreams.

Trust me, I am telling you what I know, and have experienced for myself. When I was a young man, I didn't have a plan. I missed over ninety days of school per year, and earned bad grades. I never did my homework. I never took school seriously. Eventually, I dropped out of school.

However, when I got a vision for my life, and began to see a brighter future for myself, *everything* about my attitude changed. Shortly after returning to school, I set a goal to graduate from high school; I graduated from high school. I had a dream to one day go to college; I graduated from college. I had a dream to go to earn a master's degree; I graduated with a master's degree. I dreamed of buying a home; I now own more than one home. I set a goal to travel the world; I have traveled to four continents. I set a goal to become a professor; I am currently working toward my Ph.D. I set a goal to fly airplanes; I now fly airplanes. I set a goal to be a faithful husband; I am very happily married. I set a goal to be a loving father; I am the father that I never had. Again, I don't write any of that to impress you; I write it to impress upon you that I planned my work, and I worked my plan. The fact is, most people don't plan to fail; they fail to plan. If you are serious about achieving your dreams, then you need a plan.

At the beginning of this chapter, I told you about my experience of driving into Nebraska even though I was trying to get to Sterling, Colorado. I got lost because I didn't have a map, and I didn't stop to ask for directions. Eventually, I made it to my desired destination, because I found a map, and asked for directions.

I wrote this chapter to help you draw out your map to success, and to encourage you to stop, determine where you are right now, and figure out what must change in order for you to begin moving in the direction of making your dreams part of your daily reality. Remember, knowledge is not power; the right application of that knowledge is power. Don't just read this and do nothing. Turn off the television, turn off the music, go to a quiet place, and write out your plan today. Your next chapter, the life you dream about is there for the taking; it's just waiting for you to show up!

I say to you again, turn the page! Take ownership of your life; commit to improving your life, and cut yourself off from any other possibility. Plan your work so you can work your plan.

CHAPTER 10

YOUR EDUCATION

To achieve your dreams, you need to turn the page, lay the proper foundation, get clear about your dreams, believe in yourself, eliminate self-sabotaging beliefs, and put together a roadmap to success. Once you have put together your draft roadmap or plan, it will probably become clear that you are lacking in some areas. During the planning process, you will probably discover that there are some things that you just don't know. That's where your education comes in.

There are two kinds of education, the kind that others give to you, and the kind that you give yourself. The first kind is the one you receive at school; the second kind is the one you get by reading books that were not assigned to you at school.

You need both kinds. In life, diplomas, degrees, and certificates tell people that you are able to finish something that you started. Pieces of paper tell people that you are disciplined, focused, and serious. They also tell people that you are educated, and that you can think for yourself. Although that is not always true, because I have met many people who have degrees but no common sense. Generally, however, a piece of paper gets your foot in the door.

I talk to many young people who say they "hate" school. They feel as though school is not related to their everyday lives. I understand how they feel, because the truth of the matter is, I used to hate school, too. I hated reading, I hated writing, and I hated math. I hated being called on in class by my teachers, because I hated being embarrassed every time I gave the wrong answer. I had to change the way I viewed school. I had to change the way I viewed books. I had to change the way I viewed math. Ultimately, I had to change the way I viewed myself.

Changing my perception was so important because I thought I wasn't as smart as the other students. They always seemed to have the right answers. They had better clothes than me, they had better things than me, and it even seemed like the teachers liked them more than me (I know for a fact some teachers did like other students more than they liked me). Even though those things were true, I had to ask myself, "If I don't take school seriously, how am I going to end up?" It didn't take me long to realize that I would end up like many people in my family who didn't take school seriously. They were working jobs that they hated, they were living in poor neighborhoods, they were living in tiny apartments, they were always fighting over money, and they always seemed miserable. Many of them were in prison, some were alcoholics, and some were addicted to drugs. I know that none of them planned on ending up that way. I also know that society makes it harder on some people than on others. However, I also made up my mind that I refused to be poor, I refused to be on drugs, I refused to be an alcoholic, I refused to live in poor neighborhoods unwillingly, and I refused to be just like a bunch of people that I had grown up around—people who drank, smoked, played dominoes, cards, and talked trash all day. Now let me be clear: I understand that a lot of those behaviors were coping mechanisms to help many of them deal with a lot of the things they were experiencing. However, as much as I loved them, I just could not fathom myself surrendering to the depression and self-destructive behaviors. I wanted more, and I was absolutely willing to fight for more. I'm not saying that many of them didn't fight. I'm simply saying that, at some point, some of them lost their fight. I saw where surrender leads people, and I refused to go there, no matter what.

I decided that even though it would be hard, I was going to take school seriously. I began seeing books as conversations waiting to be picked up. I began to see math as a game or a puzzle that needed to be figured out. I began to see homework as an opportunity to get better as a person. I began to see school as a way out of poverty, depression, and despair. Once I made that decision, I began treating my teachers better, and began developing better relationships with the adults around me. I knew that not all of them really cared about me or my success, but I also know that there were several who genuinely cared about me, and who wanted me to be my best. I developed relationships with those teachers, and to this day, I thank them for pouring much of their lives into me.

That is the kind of education that others give to you. It's the kind that leads to diplomas, degrees, and certificates.

The second kind of education is the kind that you give to yourself. You may not get a degree for this kind of education, but it certainly makes a bigger impression on you. To give yourself an education means that you don't have a teacher, instructor, professor, parent, or some authority figure holding you accountable for the books you read, and the papers you write. You don't have any quizzes, tests, midterms, or final exams to take. This is the kind of education that requires you to buy books on topics that you are interested in. It is the kind of education that causes you to stay up through the night because you are so enthralled by the things you are learning. It is the kind of education that nobody can take away from you.

When I was in college, most of the things I learned were learned from books that were not assigned to me by my professors. I used to complete my assignments for class, and then go to the library and stay there for hours, reading books about rhetoric, argument, philosophy, English, Spanish, geography, politics, law, and society. I became a student whose thirst for wisdom and knowledge was so insatiable that I would often stay at the library until two or three in the morning, even when school was out of session. I often went to bookstores, and just looked through every section, trying to find something that could help me become a better, more knowledgeable person. To this day, I love books, and I have thousands of them that continue to inspire me, sharpen me, and equip me to make a difference in the world.

Although I have degrees, I recognize that what is more important than the degrees is the knowledge that the degrees symbolize and represent.

Remember this: degrees may get you in the door, but only education and character can keep you there. That's why I tell people to take school seriously. The piece of paper tells people that you are worth taking a chance on. To be sure, some of the smartest people I know never went to school, and didn't graduate from college. As smart as they are, many of them have said to me that they regret not taking school more seriously, because their lack of formal education limited the kind, and amount, of opportunities they were given.

The fact is, the more school you attend, the more knowledge and wisdom you get, and the more choices you get. Usually, the more you learn, the better your grades, which means you get more acceptance letters from colleges and universities. The more colleges that accept you, the more options you have to attend the best school. Furthermore, the better the school you attend, the better job offers you will get after you graduate. The better the job offers you get after you graduate mean more money, perks, and privileges for you. Therefore, those who take school seriously usually end up with more freedom of choice, and more money in the bank.

What am I saying? You need to take school seriously by going to class, by paying attention to your teachers, by asking questions, doing your homework before you hang out with friends, and visiting your counselors to get their advice.

Now, I am fully aware that going to school, and getting a safe and secure job, is not as simple as it used to be. Now, with the changes in our economy, it is sometimes wiser to get the education you need in order to start your own business. My point is this: whether you want to be given a job or you want to create your own job, you need to take your education seriously.

ASSIGNMENT #10
YOUR EDUCATION

What are the last three books you read? Why did you read them? Were they assigned to you by a teacher? What is one thing you will do, starting today, to take your education more seriously? Now go do it!

CHAPTER 11
YOUR GRADES

When I was in elementary, middle, and high school, I was a terrible student. I had a bad attitude, missed a lot of school, and earned very bad grades. The first semester of my freshman year in high school, I earned 3 Fs, 3 Ds, and a C—that was a 0.6. Grade Point Average. However, my sophomore year, I earned 5 As and 2 Bs.

How did I go from Fs and Ds to As and Bs? I did seven things that you can do, too, if you want to improve your grades.

1. Make a decision to pick up your grades.

I made up my mind that I wanted better grades, and that I was willing to work hard to get better grades. In the same way, the first step to picking up your grades is making a decision that you want better grades, and that you are willing to work to get better grades. If you do not make that decision, then nothing else will matter.

What does it mean to make a decision? Making a decision means you pick one thing over another. It is you picking your grades over girls. It is picking your books over boys. It means picking school over sports, and picking studying over socializing.

The Latin word for decision really helps us understand what I'm trying to say. In Latin, when you make an IN-cision, you "cut into something;" but when you make a DE-cision, you "cut away from something." When you decide that you want better grades, you are deciding to cut away from anything that will keep you from getting better grades. You decide to cut away from the wrong people. To cut away from bad habits. To cut away from ANYTHING and ANYONE that could get in the way of you achieving your goal.

Who or what do you need to "cut away from" today in order to get better grades?

2. Get 8-9 hours of sleep at night.

When I was growing up, my mother used to tell me to go to bed at nine or ten o'clock at night, and then she would go to her room, and go to sleep. I would wait until I knew she was asleep, and then I would get out of bed, turn on the T.V., get on the phone, or play video games ... sometimes until three or four in the morning! How do you think I felt when it was time for me to wake up two hours later at 6 a.m.? Do you think I felt like going to school? Of course not! I started making up reasons to not go to school, and eventually I started ditching school. Because of my decision to stay up late, and disobey my mother, my grades started to drop. I don't want you to be like I was.

Get enough sleep at night. It is hard to do anything well if you are tired physically or mentally. When you stay up late even though you have to get up early the next morning, you are setting yourself up for mediocrity. When you are tired, your whole day becomes a challenge.

But if you discipline yourself to go to bed at night early enough to get a good night's sleep, you will be much more alert, and sharp, to do whatever you need to do for the day.

3. Wake up at least two hours before school.

I exercise in the morning, and while I am exercising, or eating breakfast, I ask myself several questions that help me start off my day with the right attitude. One of the most important questions I ask is, "Manny Scott, what are you grateful for today?" I take several minutes to think about all of the things and people that I am grateful for. The more I think about it, the better I begin to feel.

Another question I ask is, "What is the one thing I can do today to feel productive?" I then think about all of the things on my plate, and try to prioritize my to-do list, and make sure I put my most important items at the top of my list. These two questions help me to focus on the most important things going on in my life at any given moment.

If you want to pick up your grades, make sure you don't just roll out of bed, and go straight to school. If you're like me, it takes a little while for my body to wake up. I encourage you to wake up a couple hours before school starts so you can eat breakfast, and get your mind and body ready for a great day.

4. Arrive at class early because early is on-time, and on-time is late.

Growing up, when I did go to school, I used to be late to school at least once a week. It was a sign of my lack of respect for school, and my lack of self-control. I did not leave my house early enough to get to school on time. As a result of my being late, my grades and my relationships with my teachers were affected. Don't be like I used to be!

Wake up early, and get to class on time so you can make sure you learn everything you are supposed to learn for the day. Your teachers have worked hard to help you learn, but if you are not in class, or you are often late, you miss out on a great opportunity to learn something that will probably be on your homework or a test.

5. Pay attention when you are in class.

One of the most important things you can do to pick up your grades is pay attention to what your teacher is talking about. Pay full attention. Even if some of the material is boring to you, do your best to pay attention. One of the ways to be fully engaged in your class is to ask a lot of questions. If you don't understand something, raise your hand and ask the teacher to explain it again for you. Ask your teacher to give you an example of what he or she is talking about. Or, raise your hand, and tell the teacher you would like to summarize what he or she has just said in your own words. Then give it a try, and ask, "is that correct?" or "Is that what you're saying?" More often than not, your teacher will be glad to answer your questions, because it tells him or her that you are listening, and that you want to get good grades. Teachers love it when their students are engaged.

6. Finish your homework before you turn on the T.V., the radio, play games, get on the phone, or hang out with your friends.

After you get out of school, make sure you decide that finishing your homework is much more important than anything else you want to do. Once you get home, you might eat a snack or something, but make sure you do not turn on the television, listen to the radio, get on the phone, and certainly do not go outside and hang out with your friends. Those things can wait.

Find you a nice, quiet place to study. Make sure the lighting is good, and that you don't have things around you that can distract you.

After you get into the habit of doing your homework first, you will get faster, and better, at doing it. And, in time, you will be able to finish future homework assignments early. Imagine being done with your math homework for the entire week, and it's only Tuesday. That means you can get ahead in all your other classes too. Then you can really have fun and do other things that are of interest to you.

7. Ask for help when you need it. (Swallow your pride.)

There are going to be times when you do not understand something. That is okay and perfectly normal. It's called life! Don't beat yourself up about it. Instead, humble yourself, and ask an adult to help you. Maybe your parents can help you, or a teacher, or even a tutor. I used to go to a tutor every day for a while, because I needed help.

If you need help, please be sure to ask for it. I recommend you copy these steps, and put it in your folder, or put it in your locker, or put it on your bedroom door. I don't care where you put it, but put it somewhere that you go often, so you can be reminded of the seven steps.

I made these seven steps a part of my daily routine, and saw my grades improve a great deal. I went from Fs and Ds to As and Bs in just a few months. You can do it too.

ASSIGNMENT #11
YOUR GRADES

How are you doing in these seven areas? In which of the seven areas do you need to make the most improvement? Now, decide that you will make those improvements starting right now. Get to work.

CHAPTER 12
YOUR WORDS

Just as clothes tell people about your mind, your vocabulary also influences how people see you. People judge you by the words that come out of your mouth. Those who speak proper English sound more educated and focused than those who do not speak proper English. When you have learned to master the English language, it no longer masters you. When you speak, you should seek to express your ideas in clear and cogent ways. When you do so, you will be more understood, persuasive, and successful. Also, those who speak proper English are more marketable to corporate America, and will usually make more money, have more self-confidence, and enjoy more freedom.

It might be good for you to listen to vocabulary CDs or MP3 programs to learn new words. When I was in college, I used to walk around with headphones on so I could listen to vocabulary tapes. I wanted to learn as many new words I as I could. When I worked jobs that allowed me to wear headphones, I used to listen to vocabulary tapes while I worked. If they did not allow me to wear headphones, I used to wait for my breaks, and listen to the vocabulary tapes during my breaks. Then, when I got off work, on my way home, whether by train, or by car, or by foot, I listened to those audio tapes some more. I wanted to expand my vocabulary. I remember learning words like penury, and munificence, and reticent, and clandestine. I felt empowered to express myself more clearly with my new words. New words can do the same for you.

Also, I want to share something with you about profanity. Cussing, or profanity, is merely the reflection of a weak, foolish mind trying to express itself forcibly. Cussing is merely an indication that you haven't learned enough words to express yourself intelligently. Whenever I hear someone using profanity, I feel bad for them, because they are revealing to the world that they have an untrained mind. They are telling the world that they have not taken the time to develop their vocabulary enough to express what they would really like to say. Outside of the realm of comedy and entertainment, I rarely see profanity ever being effective. In most settings, it makes you look like an undisciplined fool.

What is important for you to remember is that you need to speak the language of your intended audience. If you are around your family, then you can use slang, and speak in a vernacular that is very casual. If you are around associates or others that you are not friends with, then you can speak in a middle-voice in which there is less slang, and is more grammatically correct. If you are speaking to professors or officials, or dignitaries, then you must learn to use language even more masterfully. What I am trying to say is that you must learn to be multi-lingual, able to speak slang, ebonics, proper English, Spanish, your native language, and anything in between. It all depends on your audience.

One way for you to master your ability to communicate is to listen to, and learn from, those who communicate clearly and properly. In ancient schools of rhetoric, students first learned how to emulate the style of great orators. They studied a variety of great speakers, and eventually found their own styles. You can do the same thing.

Learn some new words; and, once you learn those words, practice using them in sentences and in your daily conversations. You may want to keep a journal of your thoughts, read a lot of books, and pay attention to how great authors use words.

Also, when you speak, be mindful of how loud you are speaking. The volume of your voice should not be so high that everyone around you can hear everything you have to say, even though you are only talking to one person. When you are in a restaurant, the tables around you ought not hear what you are talking about. The same goes when you are at the movies, or on a cell phone. When you are loud, you are being inconsiderate of other people who are around you, who did not do anything to deserve to hear all of your business.

ASSIGNMENT #12
YOUR VOCABULARY

What is the definition of circumlocution? What is a voracious reader? What does it mean to be an autodidact? What is an eponym? What is an allusion? What is hypophora? A hypothetical question? What is chiasmus? Antimetable? Parataxis? Parallelism? Get to work.

I visited a juvenile detention center not too long ago and spoke to some young men about decision-making. One of the young men told me that he was going to be getting out of jail soon. I asked him about his plans after prison, and he told me that he was going to probably go hang out with his friends—the same friends with whom he used to gang-bang. I asked him if they were the ones he was hanging out with before he got locked up. He said, yes. I then asked him how many of them had written him letters, or visited him. He said none of them had. I asked him how many of them had checked in with his mother while he was locked up. Again, he said none of them had. I then asked him the obvious question: are they really your friends? He realized that he needed to make some important decisions about those he called friends.

Everyone in your life is either a wing or a weight. Your friends should be your wings, not your weights. Wings lift you up, and help you fly higher; weights hold you down, and limit your potential. A true friend will never ask you to do anything that would get you in trouble.

The truth is, you are a reflection of the company you keep. I once heard someone say to me, "you are a reflection of your five closest friends." I think that is true. If you have friends who are slackers, smoke weed, have bad tempers, are disrespectful to those in authority, then I would not doubt that you have some of those same characteristics yourself. If your friends are all over-weight, or broke, or miserable, or underemployed, chances are you will be chunky, broke, unhappy, and underemployed too. You are a reflection of the company you keep.

Friends are those with whom you have a mutual attraction or respect. You are usually most influenced by those with whom you have something in common. When someone influences you, you become more and more like him or her, whether you choose to or not. It often just happens unconsciously. That's what conformity is about. It is being shaped and molded by the habits, behaviors, and thoughts of your environment.

When I was younger, many of my friends used to do drugs, drink, steal, curse, fight, waste time, and disrespect women. I was just like them. To be sure, I looked up to those guys. I wanted to be just like them. I glorified "thug life," and believed that going to prison was something that would give me street credibility. Not all of them were inherently bad people; as I look back, I realize that they were just lost, looking for peace and security in their own lives. Nonetheless, it wasn't until I started to distance myself from them that I realized how dangerous and unhealthy those behaviors really were, and how blind I was to my own ignorance.

If you want to be great, you have to surround yourself with friends and associates who can sharpen you, and make you better. To find the right people to hang with, you need to evaluate your friends by asking yourself which ones are going in the same direction as you. If there are people in your life who are not serious about growing or being great, then cut them off. I know that sounds harsh, but it is true. I am not saying abandon them as much as I am saying, they can no longer occupy much of your time. If there are people in your life who aren't progressing with you, then you need to reconsider that relationship. In reality, you need to spend more time with those who make you better.

To be sure, I am not saying that you can never be around people who are not as "successful" as you, because the truth of the matter is that you need to be around people who have not enjoyed the same privileges and opportunities as you. Why? So that you can help them, and encourage them. Having said that, though, you need to be careful that you don't adopt any thoughts, attitudes, habits, or behaviors that bring you down, and cause you to settle for less than your very best.

Also, I believe that if you have a "friend" whom you always have to help or encourage, but that "friend" never helps you, then I submit to you that that person is not a friend; that person is what I call ministry. They are not bad people; but they are just not your friend. Friendship is a two-way street.

A friend is someone you enjoy being around, and who enjoys being around you. A friend will not take advantage of you, or try to use you. A true friend will not try to latch onto you, and expect you to always carry them. A friend will try to help you as well. A true friend will encourage you, and give you joy, and make you laugh. A true friend will try to beat you in giving. They will not always expect you to pay for the meals. They will insist on paying for some things too.

Furthermore, you should not have to lower your standards in order to make other people feel comfortable with themselves. If other people have a problem with your success, then let it be their problem, and not yours. It's not your fault that other people are jealous of you, and envy you. It's not your fault that others haven't made the same choices as you. At the same time, though, it is not right for you to look down your nose at someone who hasn't experienced as much joy and success as you have. Never try to look too good nor talk too wise. If you are successful, and are enjoying the blessings of God, then you don't need to boast about it.

Also, try to avoid being the smartest, sharpest, wisest person in the group because you will often end up being the person that gives the most, and whom people rely on the most. If you let that happen, you will probably end up making more deposits in others without ever taking time to make deposits in yourself. You will end up being overdrawn, and without sufficient emotional "funds" to achieve your dreams.

Make sure this next chapter of your life is filled only with people who are wings and not just weights.

ASSIGNMENT #13
YOUR WINGS AND WEIGHTS

List the names of the five people you hang out with most of the time. You are a reflection of those people. Are those five people wings or weights? Do they lift you up, and hold you back? If you have any weights, what are you going to do about them? If you keep hanging out with those people, where will you be in five years? Ten years? Is that where you want to be? If not, then you have some important cutting to do.

CHAPTER 14
YOUR LOVE LIFE

I am meeting far too many people who are in unhealthy relationships. Until I finish my book on relationships, I want to just say a few words here to help you in your own quest for love.

If you remember, in the beginning of the book, where I talked about laying a proper foundation, I discussed the different Greek words for love. One word for love is *eros*, which refers to romantic, sensual love. Erotic love is the kind of love that causes you to see someone and be physically attracted to that person. Their eyes, their smile, their lips, their bodies, their walk, their swag. There is something about them that triggers emotions and feelings in you that makes you feel all funny inside. Eros love is the kind of love that gives us the warm fuzzies.

One of my favorite poems refers to eros love when it says, "your love is more delightful than wine." I don't drink wine or alcohol anymore, but I know from experience that alcohol can be intoxicating. Eros love is like alcohol; it can make you feel drunk. When Beyonce sings her song, "Drunk in Love," she is talking about eros love. Eros love is exciting, exhilarating, and beautiful.

Eros love can also be very dangerous and unhealthy. Eros love can make us so drunk that it leads us to do some things we regret. When people get drunk, they have slurred speech, they often lose their balance, have hot tempers, and have inflated egos. In the same way, if you are not careful, and you allow yourself to fall in love with someone who is not good for you, it can be dangerously intoxicating. Eros love can cause you to lose your balance in the way you make decisions. You've heard people say love is blind; well, sometimes, love will make you blind to reality. Eros love can create emotions and intimacy in you so strong that it overpowers your ability to think clearly.

I'm convinced that most marriages and relationships today fail because they are based primarily on eros love or because of pride and selfishness. In this chapter, all I want to focus on are the different types of love as they relate to relationships. In its most basic sense, eros love is superficial, selfish love because it is the kind of love that is based on what that person can do for you physically. Because of that, eros love is very shallow and incomplete. To base your relationship solely on eros love, solely on how someone looks, or how fine he or she is, or how sexy that person is, will surely set you up for failure. That kind of love never lasts. Eventually someone else will come along who is more attractive, and more fine, and more sexy, and more whatever. Eros love can also compel you to do things with someone else that you will regret later, and will leave you broken, hurt, and lonely.

I think the best place to start any relationships is with phileo love. Phileo love is a love that is based on friendship. It is a love that is based on commonalities, or shared interests. To be sure, you can see someone, and think they are gorgeous, and feel attracted to them (eros love); but that alone is not enough.

Just because you are physically attracted to someone does not mean that that person is good for you. You want to find out if you are compatible with that person. You want to make sure you have similar interests, and that you genuinely share compatible values about money, religion, in-laws, and children, and so on. If someone has a different set of values, they might be a beautiful, nice person, but that person is not right for you. If you do not have a common interests, then I guarantee you are going to have a lot of problems in your relationship.

Then there is agape love. That's the kind of love that is unconditional. It is others-oriented. It is based on what you can do for someone else. True love is the kind of love that inspires you to help someone else. You want to help that person grow, you want to help make that person happy; you want to help brighten that person's day. If you find someone like that, and they feel the same way about you, then you might have found someone special.

However, if you are always the one giving, but the other person is always the one expecting you to give, then that is not love. Love—true love—is about a man and woman wanting the best for one another. If you are the only one willing to work to make the other person happy, but the other person is not willing to work to bring you joy, then that person is not the right person for you.

True love, in its most beautiful form, is others-oriented. It is not selfish or proud. So, until you find someone who is willing to work as hard as you are to make the relationship work, then that person is not the right one for you.

Let me say one other thing about your love life. If you, or the person you would like to be with, is not willing to change their relationship status on social media, then that person is probably not very serious about your relationship. Someone might say, "Well, I just don't like putting my business out there on social media like that. I'm more of a private person." I have no problem with that, as long as you, or the person you are with, is consistent about that policy. However, if that person always posts information on social media, but never posts anything about you, then I would be concerned about that person's feelings for you, if I were you.

Furthermore, if that person is not willing to be open about their relationship with you, then why in the world would you be willing to share your heart, time, or body, with that person? Why would you allow yourself to be someone's secret? Raise your standards, and keep them high. Don't settle for less than true love.

My point in all of this is simple: because eros love is so powerful, intoxicating, or inebriating, don't allow yourself to settle for, or be controlled by, eros love only. You don't want to arouse or awaken eros love too soon. Eros love isn't enough to cultivate a healthy, lasting relationship. Eros love, left unchecked, can ruin your life. Eros love can cause you to have kids with someone who is not truly committed to you.

The reason I am so passionate about relationships is because I have several friends, relatives, and associates who got married because they convinced themselves that they had agape love when in fact they just had eros love. They were not in love; they were "in lust." They refused to see that they were not really compatible with one another. As a result they ended up wasting a lot of time, hurting one another, and getting a divorce. They allowed themselves to be intoxicated by, controlled by, eros love.

Because of that, I want to encourage you to be sober-minded. Be completely calm and collected; be self-controlled when it comes to dating and love. Who you date, and ultimately marry, is the second most important decision you will ever make. With the right person, life can be great; with the wrong one; it can be absolutely miserable.

ASSIGNMENT #14
YOUR LOVE LIFE

If you are dating someone right now, or have someone in mind, are you friends with that person? Really? Or is he or she just someone who is easy on the eye? Be honest with yourself. Does the person you are with really share the same values as you with regard to in-laws, money, religion, and children? If not, then seriously consider whether this is a relationship worth pursuing.

CHAPTER 15
YOUR MENTORS

Most of the world's most successful people had role models who inspired and guided them. A mentor has been there, done that, become a successful person in that industry that you want to enter. They have been down the path, and can help you get there.

It is so important that you find someone who has already achieved the results you want, find out what they are doing, and do the same thing. The fact is, if we plant the same kinds of seeds, we are going get the same kinds of results. It doesn't matter if you are black, white, Mexican, Asian, poor, rich, all or none of the above. What matters is that you accelerate your growth by learning the mentalities and methods of others who are successful at what you want to do or be.

I often hear people say, "experience is the best teacher." While I believe that experience can be one of your best teachers, I do not believe that it is always the best teacher. Yes, if you want to become masterful at something, you have to keep working at it. For example, if you want to become a great speaker, then you need to find opportunities to speak, or create them. If you want to become a great musician, then you have to constantly practice your instrument. If you want to become a great entrepreneur, then you have to work at running a business. Having said that, however, you need to remember that experience is not always the best teacher. Rather, other peoples' experience can be your best teacher.

In order to find a mentor, the first thing you need to do is figure out what type of mentor you need. There are several types of mentors that you may want to consider.

EDUCATIONAL

You want to find some teachers, administrators, and counselors in your school who can give you the guidance you need to become the person you want to one day become. I know that there are some bad teachers and administrators who do not really care about you, and who only work for a paycheck. I have had plenty of those kinds of teachers. However, I have had the privilege of being mentored by educators who really poured their lives into me.

Erin Gruwell was one of those persons. She inspired me to want more for myself. After I returned to school my sophomore year, I had ambitions to go to college, but I had no idea about what I needed to do to prepare myself for college. I didn't know about the ACT, SAT, requesting college applications, or letters of recommendation. I did not know how to write a personal statement. Fortunately, I had the privilege of meeting a twenty-three-year-old student-teacher named Erin Gruwell. Erin helped me apply to the University of California at Berkeley. She modeled for me what I needed to do and be in order to go to college.

My mother had given me the confidence, and the passion; Erin Gruwell had given me the guidance. I needed both.

If you are in school, or desire to return to school, you too need to find you an Erin Gruwell who can help give you the guidance and direction you need in order to go to the next level in your life.

FINANCIAL

You want to also find someone who can help you acquire and manage your money. If you want to be wealthy, then you should study the methods of people who are wealthy. You need to ask them what they did to become so successful. You need to find out what their habits are, their philosophies and strategies. You need help putting together a budget, and learning how to balance your checkbook. You need someone to help you think about investing in stocks, bonds, and real estate.

A couple of people who inspire me financially are Dave Ramsey, Donald Trump, Robert Kiyosaki, Napolean Hill, and many other people you probably have never heard of. All of these people are extremely wealthy, and know what it takes for others to get wealthy as well. I study books written by them, and apply many of the lessons they teach. I speak from experience when I say that what they teach actually works.

PHYSICAL

You want to also find someone to help you become more healthy. If you are not in good shape physically, then you are not going to be able to enjoy your success. Find a trainer, a coach, an athlete that you can exercise with. Find out what they eat, and what they don't eat. Find out what kinds of exercise they do, and how often they do them. Find out what their habits are so you can emulate them, and get the same results that they are getting.

RELATIONAL

You want to also find someone who is great at developing relationships. There are some people who can walk into any room, and begin a conversation with anyone, because he or she is a good at starting and building relationships. You want to learn as much as you can about how to open a conversation, how to engage people, how to build trust, and establish comfort. You want to know how to encourage other people, and build them up. You want to learn how to tend to someone who is grieving, and comfort people who are not well.

Also, you want to find someone who has the ability to help you attract your dream husband or wife. Some people have the ability to attract the most beautiful women, and some women have the ability to hook the hottest guys (not that I would know what a "hot guy" looks like). Rather than being jealous of them, you want to learn what they do to attract women or men. You want to learn how they think, how they dress, how they carry themselves, how they speak, and all the good things that go into a great relationship.

SPIRITUAL

You want to also find you someone who can help you attend to your soul. You need someone who is a spiritual mentor to ask you the hard questions about yourself. You need someone to be able to call you out by pointing out things in your life that need to be addressed. You need someone to ask you about your integrity. My mentors are older pastors or professors to whom I can go for advice, and prayer. Dr. John Woodbridge, Dr. Larry Murphy, Dr. Grant Osborne, Dr. Craig Ott, Dr. Michael Bullmore, Dr. Greg Scharf, Dr. Perry Downs, and a few others have helped me become a much better man.

FAMILIAL

You also need mentors who ask you questions like, "how are you treating your wife and kids?" "When you are away from home, who keeps you accountable?" There are a few cherished mentors in my life who ask me these hard questions, and challenge me to become a more loving husband and father.

You need older women around you to share their wisdom about life with you, and can help you become a better wife, a better mother, and a better person.

Men like the Rev. Mark Dennis, Rev. K. Edward Copeland, Rev. Dr. Robert Long, Rev. Daniel Robinson often ask me questions that challenge me to become a better family man.

PROFESSIONAL

It is so important for you to find a role model or mentor who is doing what you want to do professionally. If you want to be a lawyer, you need to find a lawyer as your mentor. If you want to be a motivational speaker, you need a mentor to guide you. If you want to be a doctor, then you need to spend time getting advice and guidance from a doctor. Whatever it is you want to do, remember that you are not the first one to do it (most of the time). Therefore, don't make things harder on yourself than they need to be.

The fact is, you do not need to try drugs to learn that they are not good for you. You don't need to go to jail in order to learn that it is somewhere you don't want to end up. You don't need to mismanage your money to learn that bankruptcy hurts. If you want to be successful, then you want to learn from the mistakes of others. Instead of reinventing the wheel, and wasting time, you can learn from others, and find out what they did in order to succeed.

In life, you want to find yourself life coaches or mentors who can bring out the best in you. You want to be influenced by people who are successful in different areas of life. Some people are stronger in, say finance, than they are in relationships. That doesn't make them a bad person; it just makes them better at finance. Get advice from them about finances, and not relationships.

I once read a proverb that says, "If you listen to constructive criticism, you will be at home among the wise." You want to find a mentor, guidance counselor, advisor, or someone who knows something about how to get from where you are to where you want to be.

There may be other people in your life that you could ask for advice right now. Maybe they are friends of your parents, your next-door neighbor, or someone else. Sometimes, the people who can help you are right around the corner from you, and are waiting for someone to ask them for their advice.

Also, I've learned that people like to talk about themselves. An elderly man that I used to visit, Mr. Willie Harris, was one hundred years old when I met him. I used to hang out with him about once a month, and learn about life from him. He had traveled the world, had seen many of the world's great monuments, and he had even ridden his bicycle from Arkansas to Ohio! He was full of stories and was a storehouse of wisdom. He once told me, "When you are in the presence of greatness, just shut your mouth and listen, because you never know what you might learn!" As direct as that may seem to you, I appreciated that lesson. I have been around many great people, and always remember to pay close attention to what they are saying. By doing so, I have never left a conversation without learning something new, and helpful, about life and success.

I didn't grow up with many positive role models. Most of the people I looked up to were seasoned criminals, con artists, hustlers, and drug users. But when I decided to take school seriously, and break the cycle of poverty, and mediocrity in my family, I began to pick up books and learned to love reading. I often went to the library and skimmed books that looked interesting, and I learned very quickly that *books are conversations waiting to be picked up.*

I have always wished that I could have met and served with the Rev. Dr. Martin Luther King, Jr., and other great people in history. I sometimes imagined what it would be like to soak up their wisdom like a sponge. Since I didn't have a time machine, I did the next best thing: I read many of the books that they had written. I used to sit down for hours and just drink from the rich fountains of their wisdom, and learn about their values, strategies, missions, and visions.

To this day, if you want to find me in my leisure time, you will probably find me in a bookstore, library, in a park, or on a bench with a book and a journal.

I have learned that success leaves clues, and you thus need to study those who have done what you want to do. You can save yourself years of experience, and mistakes, by taking the time to read about the experiences and mistakes of others. If you want to be a great singer or rapper, then you need to study the lyrics, beats, riffs, runs, and techniques of great singers and rappers; if you want to be great, you have to study, and learn from those great people who have gone before you.

ASSIGNMENT #15
YOUR MENTORS

Who has done, or is doing, what you want to do with your life? Name three or four people who are doing what you want to do, and write their names down in the margins of this book right now. Have they written any books that you can buy or check out at the library? Have they made any DVDs or CDs you can study? Have they done any interviews you can watch, and learn from? Take time to research what they have done, and make time to study them. Their hard-earned wisdom could save you a lot of time, hurt, money, and energy.

CHAPTER 16

YOUR MONEY

About ten years ago, I was invited to speak to a group of very wealthy businessmen. After my presentation, they invited me to hang out with them. For the sake of their privacy, I won't tell you who they were, or where they lived. All I will say here is that each of them made at least ten million dollars a year. Many of them made much more than that.

One of the men kindly invited me to go freshen up in his home before we went out for the night. I'll never forget walking into that man's home, which sits on the coast of the Atlantic Ocean. When I walked through his front door, I was in awe. The entrance to his home was bigger than most homes I had ever seen. There were maids working on every one of the four floors of his mansion. He had an indoor swimming pool and an outdoor one. Behind his home was a huge, luxurious yacht that was easily worth tens of millions of dollars.

At dinner that night, one of the millionaires asked me about my life. I began sharing more of my journey with the group. For some reason, I even began to share some of my own financial problems with them. I think subconsciously I reasoned that any one of them had the capacity to pull out a checkbook and write me a check that could solve all of my financial problems. In fact, I think I was hoping that one of them would do just that. However, no one wrote me a check, or offered to help me out. Instead, they just looked at me with pity. They felt sorry for me, and partied the night away. No one else really talked to me for the rest of the night.

At the end of the night, I went to my hotel room and soberly reflected on what I had done. "Why did I embarrass myself like that?" I wondered. "Why did I feel as though I needed to put my business out there like that? I sat alone in my room angry and upset by what I had just done.

That experience taught me several lessons. First, no matter how much money people have, they are not obligated to give you any of it. In fact, most people could not care less about your problems, financial or otherwise. They didn't cause your problems, and so they feel no need to help you solve your problems. After all, they are your problems, not theirs. You can tell most people about your financial "issues" all you want. Chances are they are going to just feel sorry for you, maybe pray for you, and go on with life, never really thinking about you or your problems again. In fact, they will probably avoid ever seeing you again.

I'll even take it a step further and say that your employer is not supposed to make you rich. The company you work for is not supposed to make you rich. That is not their responsibility. They pay you to help them solve their problems, and your paycheck is what you get in return. What you do with your money is none of their business. Your problems are not your boss's business.

The second, but more important, lesson I learned from that experience is that if I am every going to be financially free, then I must be willing to work for it myself. I realized that I was going to have to find my own way to be financially free, because rich people aren't just giving away money.

As a result of that experience, I decided to never put myself in that position again. I decided that I would never embarrass myself like that again. I decided that I would never put my business out there like that again. Instead, I decided that I was going to find a way to be financially free no matter what.

I began to work harder, and smarter. I learned about business, and money, and wealth. Because of all that I have learned and done over these last ten years, I can proudly say that I am doing quite well for myself.

While I am no expert on money yet, I have learned some important lessons about wealth that I would like to share with you. In this chapter, then, I want to talk to you about your money. For your development during this next chapter of your life, it is important for you to learn about the Path of Money; and, you must learn how to put together a budget that works for you.

THE PATH OF MONEY

Money flows in and out of your life like a river. In the beginning, there are really only two legal ways for you to get money: someone gives it to you or you earn it. If you have a rich relative who leaves a lot of money in his or her will, then you have something with which to work. If you are like me, however, then you are going to have to work for your money.

I have held all kinds of jobs in my life, just so I could have a little money in my pocket. I have cut grass, shoveled snow, washed cars, worked in fast food restaurants, been a security guard, a file clerk, a driver, a paperboy, and so much more. (I've even dressed up in an animal suit and danced at birthday parties for little kids.) I have never been afraid of hard work. In the same way, you are going to have to be willing to work hard to make some money.

Then, once you get that money, you need to realize that there are four choices you can make with your money. You can spend it, hold it, donate it, or invest it. This is where most people mess up. Once they get a paycheck, they spend it right away on liabilities—things that will depreciate in value over time. Once you buy those new shoes, or clothes, they begin to lose value right away. Eventually, you have little to no money left to save.

The second thing you can do with your money is save it. Instead of spending your money on things that will lose value over time, you can put that money in a bank account, and save it.

The third thing you can do is give it away. You can give to a charity, or to someone in need. You can give it to a religious or a philanthropic organization.

The fourth thing you can do with your money is invest it. To invest means to spend your money on things that will increase in value over time.

The poorest people spend most of their money, save some of it, share a little of it, and invest none of it. Wealthy people, however, spend none of it, give some of it, save a lot of it, and invest most of it.

Poor people work for money; rich people make money work for them. That's what investing is. It is putting your money in places so that it works for you.

I don't want to get too technical at this point. I'll just say at this point that if you are an investor, you can lend your money to others at an interest rate that will allow you to receive more money than you let them borrow; or, you can buy things (assets) that go up in value, which can generate cash flow, and give you some nice spending money.

If you invest wisely, your money will work for you, and you will have more money to work with. What's great about investing is that you can then take the money you have earned and re-invest it in more things so that you can receive even more money. Over time, if you work at saving and investing your money, you will have much more money to work with.

Learn about the Path of Money, and learn to put your money in places where it can work for you (businesses, real estate, stocks, mutual funds, REITs, etc.).

BUDGETING

This leads me to talk about budgeting. A budget is just a document that lets you tell your money where to go, before you even get it. In essence, it is a planning document.

Why do we use schedules and calendars? When you plan out your time, you are making decisions about what is a priority in your life. When you plan out your day, you are devoting time to the most important things in your life. And so before that day gets here, or before that month arrives, you pull out your planner, and you prioritize what matters to you, and you write it down on your calendar. When you manage your time, you are telling your time where to go. You are telling your time where you are going to spend it. A schedule, a plan, or a calendar allows you to proactively take control of where you want to invest your time.

The same thing applies to your budget. Putting together a budget is saying, "this is where my money is going to go before I even get it in my bank account." When you have that kind of plan, you are able to take control of your resources, of your financial destiny, and, of your life in general. I have learned that when you take control of your numbers—when you are clear about the money you are making and spending—you start taking control of your life.

For the rest of this chapter I want to talk very briefly with you about the budget that I have used for the last five years. It is very basic, but it has worked for me. You can create your own. It is really simple, but it is not simplistic. It is going to require hard work and discipline to really plan and implement your budget. But here is what you need to include in your budget.

1. Income. First you want to write down how much money you are making per week or per month. List how much you are making from your allowance, or from your job. Put down any money that is coming in on a regular basis, if any. If you are married, include your spouse's income as well, because you are a team; and, teamwork makes the dream work. I have a column for every month of the year, and in that column, I put how much money I am scheduled to make per month. Then at the far right, I add up all my projected income, and total it.

2. Expenses. Second, you want to list your regular expenses. How much you pay for housing. How much you pay for your electricity. Your phone bills. Your water and sanitation bills. You include all your household expenses. Your Internet bills, your cable bills. You want to include your expenses related to lawn-care if you have a yard. You need to also include your transportation expenses. How much do you pay for your car note? How much do you pay for your insurance? For fuel? For maintenance? You also need to include your expenses for your clothing and grooming. How much do you need to spend on clothing? How much on haircuts or going to the salon? How much will you spend on dry cleaning?

3. Savings. Save about 10% of every paycheck you receive. Determine how much you are going to save from every check you receive. You know I believe in paying yourself first, paying your bills, and then giving a gift, or charity to help other people.

4. Taxes. If you are self-employed, be sure to put aside money for taxes. Put 15-25% of your check in a bank account for taxes. Trust me, it will come back and bite you in your behind if you have not put money aside. I had to pay a lot of money in taxes one year because I did not put that money aside. I got hit with this huge bill, and it frustrated me to no end. I was so upset. I could not believe that I had to give the government tens of thousands of dollars of money that I earned. But, because I didn't really understand how taxes work, I didn't plan to pay anyone back. Learn from my mistake, and put aside 15-25% of every check you get. Most importantly, find out how much you will be expected to pay back in taxes.

5. Emergency Fund. Save up enough money in an emergency fund to pay 3-6 months of your monthly bills. You can look at all of these financial gurus and they'll tell you, you should have an emergency fund. So, get yourself an emergency fund. Some people say get started off with a thousand dollars and only use that for emergency expenses. Other financial advisors say you should have three months of your monthly expenses saved up. Some say six months. Some say eight months. The point is, save up for a rainy day. A difficult time will come (a death in the family, a last-minute flight, a medical bill, a car breaks down), and you want to have money to help you offset the costs of the emergency.

6. Insurance. Insurance is one of those things that is better to have and not need, than to need and not have. In life, accidents happen. Someone gets sick, or needs dental work, or gets into a car accident. Sometimes, people close to you die. Insurance is, in essence, security for you and your family. It reduces your expenses when accidents do happen. Because of that, I recommend you at least get medical, dental, automobile, and life insurance for you and those closest to you.

7. Credit Card Debt. It is true that the borrower is servant to the lender. Those who loan you money have a certain degree of control over you. If you have credit cards, then you are not completely free. I highly encourage you to pay off your credit card debt as soon as is practicable. Write down how much do you expect to pay on each card per month, and I recommend the snowball method, where you pay off as much as you can; and, once you pay off the largest sum or lowest sum or whatever you choose, use that money that you would have spent on that other credit card bill to pay off another credit card debt. Keep doing that until you get out of debt. My wife and I used the snowball method, which Dave Ramsey recommends. As a result, we were able to eliminate all of our credit card debt.

8. Invest. Learn as much about money as you can. This chapter is providing you with the most fundamental aspects of money management. You would do well to invest in books that will teach you more about managing your money, and especially about investing your money. My wife and I have made some pretty good investments, and we have been able to reap some of the rewards from them. You want to get to the place where you are not working for money, but your money is working for you.

In conclusion, this is how I have budgeted my money for the last several years. Every month, about a week before the month is over, I sit down and plan out my budget for the next month. If it were December, I would begin planning for my January budget during the second or third week of December.

How exactly do I do that? I pull out a pencil and I write down on a blank piece of paper how much money I expect to bring in for the month. I list out all of my expected income for January. Then I write down my anticipated expenses for January.

I put 10% in savings; 10% for giving; 70% for living expenses, and then 10% for discretionary spending (take my wife out on a date; take my kids to the movies; buy my kids some toys; save for a vacation, etc.).

I always determine how much money I have left, and think carefully about what I should do with that money. Should I save it for February, and use it for some expenses there? Should I put a little more on this month's credit card bill? Should I pay more on my car note or my mortgage? Should I add it to my emergency fund?

Once you have covered your living expenses, your food, your transportation, and your grooming, ask yourself, "what's the best, most important thing I should do with this money?"

My wife and I have essentially followed the above plan, and it has been working. My wife and I had to sit down and work these things out together. We manage our money together. We manage our budget together. I put the plan together, and I talk it through with her. Then she gives me her feedback and she tells me where she thinks we need to make adjustments.

As a result of our working together, we have been able to get so much more done. You can do more together than you can do alone. Make sure you do it together. If you will do that my friend you will better position yourself to be free. But it is going to take work and sacrifice.

I share this information with you about budgeting because I know firsthand that it is no fun being broke. It's no fun having more month than money. Make sure you are putting a little something away for a rainy day.

Also, make sure you are sticking to your budget. At the end of the month, look at it. How did you do? Did you stick to it? Look at your bank account. Look online, if you have online banking. How much did I actually spend compared to how much I budgeted to spend? Did I go over? Did I go under?

Maybe I need to eat at home more often, instead of eating out so much. This would save us some money.

If you spend a lot of money eating out, or on clothes, you are wasting money that you could be using to become financially free. Work that budget, for it contains your plan. So plan your work and work your plan! My friend, I have been able to knock out all my credit cards.

Debt limits you. It shackles you. It inhibits you. It prevents you from living out your dreams. Work to free yourself from all debt. You should just make up your mind that you are going to be financially free. Make up your mind that you are not going to be a slave to debt. That you are not going to be a slave to poverty. Make up your mind that you are going to do what you need to do to manage your money well so you can be completely free. Take control of your life by taking control of your money. You do that my friend and you will be financially free.

One of my mottos in my household is the Scott family is "faithful and free." I am going to be faithful to God. Faithful to my wife. I am going to be a faithful father. I am going to be a faithful steward over the resources I have been given; and, I am going to be free. I am going to be free mentally, emotionally, physically, financially, and spiritually. I am going to be completely free, so that I can live to my fullest potential, and help many more people.

I want you to do the same, but it is going to take you being disciplined with your money. I want you to be free financially, but it is going to take work. It is going to take sacrifice, but I can tell you that it is working for my family. I am living the kind of life that I have always dreamed about. My friend, I am more free now than I have ever been, and I am becoming more free day-by-day.

ASSIGNMENT #16
CREATE YOUR OWN BUDGET

Your assignment from this chapter is to put together a budget for yourself, for your family, or for your business. Include income and expenses and totals; do it just for this month—maybe you can do it for the next couple of months—and determine how you can save more than you spend. That will be key for your financial freedom.

Eventually I want you to have a budget for the entire year. When you start getting more income, it is nice to just have a budget 12 months out. I have included a budget template below. It's very basic, but it can at least give you an example of what my budget sheet looks like. You can use it, improve upon it, or create one of your own. Like I said, the main thing is that you take control of your money so that your money doesn't take control of you. Free yourself from the bondage of financial frustration, and write a new financial chapter in your life.

BUDGET: JANUARY	
INCOME	
Allowance	$
Job(s)	$
Total Income	$
EXPENSES	
Savings	$
Taxes	$
Rent	$
Electricity, Water, Garbage	$
Phone, Internet	$
Food/Groceries	$
Transportation	$
Clothing	$
Grooming	$
Insurance	$
Total Expenses	$
Net (Income-Expenses)	$

CHAPTER 17
YOUR MORNINGS

You probably could not tell by looking at me now that I used to play football in high school and college. In fact, throughout high school, I won a few all-state awards in football and track. Over the years, while playing on several different teams, I have noticed that every team has at least two groups of people on it.

There are those who are on the team so they can wear the uniform, attract guys or girls, get into games for free, or some other reason. People in this group stand out because, during practices, they are the ones slacking off, they usually complain the most, give up the fastest, make a bunch of excuses, and ultimately end up on the bench. People in this group gossip about what is wrong with the team, but don't do anything to make the team better. These people are mediocre at best.

The second group of people, however, is just the opposite. They are the ones who are focused during practice. They push themselves to their limit. They are the ones working during the off-season, running routes, shooting baskets, doing cheers, lifting weights, watching tape, listening to the coaches, studying their opponents, and sharpening their game. People in this second group do not want to settle for merely being on the team; they want to win. As a result, they take action to get better every day.

In life, those who are successful don't just *look* the part, but they make sure they *are* the part. In order to achieve your dreams, you must not only envision your destination, plan your route to get there, you must be a person of action! You must do a little bit every day to execute your plan—to bring your dreams closer to your reality. Specifically, what kind of things do you need to do in order to make massive movement toward the achievement of your dreams?

Let's start at the very beginning. Let's start with your morning. You need to make sure you start your day off on the right foot. How can you go through each day feeling great, no matter what challenges you may be facing? I've learned some invaluable lessons that I'd like to share with you to help you make the most of every day.

First, you need to know that the questions you ask yourself determine what you focus on.

Do a quick activity with me. It'll take no more than thirty seconds to complete:

• Take about ten seconds to look around the room that you're in right now. What things in the room are RED? Stop reading right now, and look around. No, really STOP READING and FIND THE RED!

• Now, for the next ten seconds, (after you finish reading the next two sentences, of course) please close your eyes , and with your eyes closed (no cheating), point at everything red in the room. Do it for 10 seconds, then open your eyes, and keep reading.

• Now, after you finish reading this sentence, please close your eyes again, and with your eyes closed, try to point at everything in the room that is brown. NO CHEATING!

If you really did the exercise, you probably had no problem pointing to the red things in the room. But when I asked you to point to all the brown things, a little high-pitched voice in your head probably responded, "Brown!? You asked me to look for everything that was red, not brown!"

If you are like me, you had a hard time pointing to the brown things in the room. But why? Because the question I asked you (where are the red things?) determined what you were looking for (red things). My question caused your mind to focus on the things in the room that were red, AND, consequently, my question caused your mind to ignore everything else in the room that was not red. The questions you ask yourself determine what you focus on.

You still with me? Good. Now let's take in one step further.

Second, what you focus on determines how you feel at any given moment. A little while ago, I was scheduled to speak 29 times in 16 states in three weeks. One day, halfway through the tour, after speaking several times, I drove over three hours to catch a couple flights that lasted a few more hours. After the airline informed me they had lost my luggage, I drove another hour to my hotel. I did not get to sleep until 4:30 a.m.! I set my alarm to wake me up at 5:45 a.m, so I could go speak to four large groups.

I have a question for you? When my alarm started screeching at 5:45 a.m., how do you think I felt? After getting only an hour and fifteen minutes of sleep, I felt terrible. I did not feel like speaking. My body was tired, my brain was tired. I was exhausted. "Why?" "Why did I do this to myself?" "Why did I schedule these events so close together?" I wallowed there in my bed feeling something awful. The questions I was asking myself made me focus on things that made me feel even worse. What you focus on determines how you feel at any given moment.

I have some important questions for you: How do you feel most of the time? Depressed? Sad? Lonely? Angry? Unappreciated? Picked on? Is it possible that some of the questions you ask daily are causing you to focus on things that are making you feel terrible? Miserable? Sad?

Furthermore, is it possible that your questions are causing you to focus on things that may be setting you up for failure? Are your questions setting you up for failure before you get out of bed in the morning? Before you even leave the house? Are your questions setting you up for failure on your job? At school? In your relationships?

Before you walk into work or school in the morning, do you ask yourself, "I wonder who is gonna act crazy today?" Or "Why do I have to work with (insert person's name here)?" Or, "Why can't I get more money for doing this crappy job?" Or—you get the point. If those are your questions, your mind is going to focus on things that do not help you. Those questions do not empower you. They do not make you feel better about yourself, your co-workers, your classmates, or your job.

What can you do to feel better about yourself and your life? Questions are the answer. If you want to change how you feel, you need to change your questions.

When I was lying in that bed at 5:45 a.m., I knew that I was going to be speaking to four audiences NO MATTER HOW I FELT. So, in order to put myself in the right state of mind to be my best for the day, I did what I'm telling you to do: I started asking better questions.

Here are some questions asked myself that morning (and my answers):

What am I grateful for today?
I am grateful to be alive today; I am grateful for health; I am grateful I heard that alarm clock; I am grateful I have an opportunity to work; I am grateful I have a sound mind.…

Who loves me today, and who do I love?
My wife loves me, my children love me, my mom loves me, my friends love me, my brothers love me; and I love them.

What am I proud about in my life today?
I am proud to be a great father. I am proud to be at this place in my life, doing well. I am proud that I lost 35 pounds.

What is the most important thing I need to get done today?
I need to connect with these four audiences, helping them realize their own potential and power to change their own lives and the lives of those around them.

And so on. What about you? What are some questions you can ask to change how you feel, and empower you to have a great day? What are some questions you can ask yourself every morning? In the afternoon? After a challenging experience? You can use my questions as a starting point, and think up some of your own. Here are some examples of questions you can ask yourself:

EMPOWERING QUESTIONS
What is one thing I can do today to enjoy myself?
Who can I help today?
What can I do to make someone else's day a little brighter?
Or, even when you face challenges, you can ask empowering questions like: Even though I might be sick, what am I grateful for today?
Even though I do not have a job, what can I do to put myself in position to get a job?
Even though I do not have a car, what can I do to make it to that meeting or interview on time?
Even though I do not have a lot of money, what am I thankful for today?

Your questions are only limited by your imagination. No matter where you are in your life, I encourage you to write your questions down somewhere, and answer them every morning. Get into a habit of asking and answering these questions. By doing so, you will begin seeing life through new eyes, and, more importantly, you will begin to feel much better about life. A little diet and daily exercise wouldn't hurt either.

ASSIGNMENT #17
YOUR MORNING RITUAL

Currently, what is your morning ritual? Do you just roll out of bed in the morning without properly preparing yourself for the day ahead? What are some things you are going to begin doing from this day forward?

CHAPTER 18

YOUR RESPONSIBILITY

There is a young man that I have had the privilege of working with, and who seemed to have every disadvantage: His father died in his arms (from gang violence); his mother is an alcoholic, addicted to drugs, and he was a high school drop-out. Rather than making excuses for the cards that life dealt him, this young man returned to school to get his GED, and he recently enrolled in college. It takes him an hour to get to school on public transportation, and an hour to get home after he leaves the library. About a month after school had been in session, I asked him how he was doing in school. He said that he was doing well, but that he didn't have any books for his classes. He couldn't afford to buy them. I asked him how he had been keeping up with his homework assignments, and he told me that he had been staying in the library until his homework was finished, sometimes leaving campus at nine or ten o'clock at night.

Rather than making an excuse about why he couldn't complete his homework, this young man went to the library every night to use the books in the library. Why? He had taken responsibility for his life. He didn't blame his teachers for giving him homework. He didn't blame his mother for being on drugs. He didn't even blame society for the fact that he couldn't afford books. Instead, he took ownership of his situation, and decided to change it. I was so pleased to discover that because of his hard work, this young man received a full scholarship that pays for all of his college tuition and books.

That young man turned the page, and took responsibility for his life. To take responsibility means to recognize that you have the power to choose how you will respond to whatever comes your way. In between every action and your response to that action is a space—a gap—where you have the power to decide how you are going to respond. After the stimulus, and before your response to that stimulus, you have the power to make a choice about how you are going to handle or address the situation.

In other words, taking responsibility means that you don't blame anyone else for the results you have received or the situation you are in. Those who take responsibility for their lives refuse to make excuses about why something didn't work. Rather, they are proactive, meaning they don't wait for things to happen to them; they make things happen for them. As a result, they usually get better results than those who are merely reactive.

I think it is important for me to say something here, very briefly, about the reality of evil, institutionalized racism, and systemic injustice in the world today. I have lived through some really difficult circumstances that were largely caused by racism, poverty, and systemic evil. I grew up in neighborhoods where the police used to abuse us and harass us, even when we weren't doing anything wrong. I have been thrown on the hoods of many police cars and called some really mean, racist things, even though I was minding my own business. That kind of stuff is still happening in our world right now. There are some people who are living in slavery right now. There are systems in place that make it harder for some people to get access to quality schools, good jobs, adequate healthcare, and decent housing. Any educated person readily admits this.

In light of those realities, when I speak of taking responsibility, I am talking about doing something proactive about those situations. I am talking about fighting harder to improve your life. Working harder to get your education. Working harder to fight for those who do not have equal opportunities in our world. The alternative is to cry and become depressed about those things. I don't believe that crying or feeling sorry for myself are options I can live with. I choose to fight. I choose to work. I choose to do everything in my power to address those situations. I choose to take responsibility; and, I do so by starting with me.

I believe that if I want to change the world, that I must first clean up my own room. I have enough problems in my own life that need my attention. Once I have honestly addressed those, then I can broaden my concerns. Taking responsibility in this way also gives you a little more credibility when addressing other, more complicated issues.

With that said, to make sure that the next chapters of your life are great, begin by taking responsibility for your life. Work on your life. Work on improving your shortcomings. Refuse to make excuses about why you are where you are in life, and instead take matters into your own hands and turn the page! Then, you can go on and change the world.

ASSIGNMENT #18
YOUR RESPONSIBILITY

What are some problems in the world that you would like to address? Are you bothered or budded by global poverty, aids, racism, or injustice? What is one thing you would like to do to become a part of the solution to those problems? Is there anything in your personal life that would disqualify you from speaking up about any of those issues? Is there anything in your personal life that could damage your credibility? If so, identify those things, and begin addressing them, or eliminating them, right away.

CHAPTER 19

YOUR TIME

Ralph Waldo Emerson once said, "This time, like all times, is a very good one, if we know what to do with it." What he was saying is that you need to use your time wisely. It is so easy to think you have all the time in the world, especially if you are young, but the reality is that you only have so much time at your disposal.

Those who maximize the use of their time usually get better results because they have focused their energies on accomplishing one thing as opposed to several things. They have learned to exert themselves on things that will get them closer to achieving their goals. The fact is, those who maximize the use of their time usually enjoy more credibility and influence among their friends and associates, which almost always translates into more success.

I remember hearing Oprah Winfrey describe the time when her personal trainer confronted her. She hired him because she wanted to lose weight, but she had developed a habit of showing up late to her workout sessions with him. At first, her trainer was gracious, and gave her the benefit of the doubt for her lateness. But after Oprah was late a few more times, he confronted her saying, "my time is just as valuable as yours, so don't waste it!" Her trainer recognized that time is very important, and he wanted to make sure that he maximized every moment.

In life, you must learn to maximize your use of time by refusing to procrastinate. Many people don't realize that busyness is a form of laziness. It is easy to stay busy doing something, convincing ourselves that we are maximizing our use of time, when in actuality we are doing something that we shouldn't be doing, in order to avoid doing what we ought to be doing. In other words, *it doesn't matter what you do, if it's not what you are supposed to be doing.*

For example, have you ever needed to complete a homework assignment, or chores, but in order to avoid doing them, you did something else to stay busy? You rationalized your way out of doing what you needed to do. Rather than busying yourself with things that are not a priority, you have to learn to focus your energies on only those things that can help position you for success.

How do you do that? Every Sunday, I like to sit down at my desk, and write out my plan for the week, and schedule things that must get done that week. I make sure I put my most significant responsibilities on my schedule first, so that I don't bog my schedule down with other things that are less important. If I don't put my most important things in my schedule first, then my schedule will be too full for the goals, objectives, and action steps that would move me closer to my dreams.

Furthermore, almost every morning I ask myself, "what do I want most out of life?" Then I ask myself, "what do I want least in life?" Then, I ask, "what must I do today in order to get me closer to what I want most, and what must I do today to keep me from what I want least?" That simple exercise of asking yourself questions can help you focus your time and energy for the day. You may also want to ask, "what five things can I be thankful for today?" That is often a good way to focus your mind, and warm your heart for a day of massive action and total fulfillment.

If you are serious about achieving your dreams, then you will use your time wisely. You won't show up late for important appointments. You won't waste three or four hours watching videos and learning new dance moves (unless you want to be a dancer or something—but even then you should be practicing more than watching others). Your time needs to be spent getting better at what you want to do with your life. Why? Because you want to be the best that you can be, and you ultimately become what you think about most of the time. So make sure you are focusing your mind on, and investing your time in, your dreams, goals, objectives, and action steps so that you can get closer, and not further, from the life of your dreams.

ASSIGNMENT #19
YOUR PRIORITIES

Busyness is a form of laziness. Is there anything in your life that you have been allowing to keep you busy? Sit down, and write out your schedule for the next seven days. Put the most important things on your schedule first. Prioritize your priorities. Then, and only then, can you include other, less important things on your schedule.

CHAPTER 20
YOUR APPEARANCE

People make their minds up about you within the first three seconds of meeting you. The fact is, how you dress influences what people think about you. Therefore, the better you dress, the better your first impression, which results in better relationships, more opportunities, and often more money. I know that is shallow, but it's true. God looks at our hearts; people look at our appearance.

There was a show on MTV a while ago called *From G's to Gents*, and it emphasizes the importance of appearance and presentation. Farnsworth Bentley, the show's host, takes guys who have thug-life tendencies and wardrobes, and tries to transform them into men of distinction. Those who do not make the transformation well end up getting kicked off the show. In life, people are judging you based on your appearance, and although you may not be on a television show, you can just as likely lose an opportunity because of how you dress.

The fact is your clothes are a reflection of your mind and maturity. If you are hanging with your friends, then dress however you like. But if you want to work for a successful company, then you need to know that they are evaluating you to see if you would be a good person to represent their company's values, mission, and vision.

I used to walk around with my pants sagging. It was always hard to run. I couldn't run very fast because I had to keep pulling up my pants, or use one hand to hold them up. I'm all for the freedom of expression in how people dress, but I also believe that sagging pants are often symbolic of one who is moving very slowly toward their goals. Unless they are entertainers, I rarely see a reason for someone to be walking around with their pants sagging, and their underwear showing.

How then are you supposed to dress for corporate America? If you are a male, then you need to get you some dress slacks and a button-down dress shirt. If you can afford it, buy a suit and tie, and a nice black pair of dress shoes. Ladies, please, please, please find clothes that are appropriate for a business environment. I tell you this because nobody told me, and I wore some clothes to work that were very inappropriate for a corporate environment.

Remember, gold teeth are a no-no, and tattoos are not helpful. If you are going to get tattoos, put them on places that won't be a distraction to other people with whom you will interact on your job. Unkempt hair is not cute, and you should avoid hairstyles that can be a distraction. If you have pimples or zits, then get some Proactive or something to fix your problem (it will help your self-esteem too). Also, your pants need to be around your waist, so get a size that fits your waist, and a belt to hold them up. Remember, your underwear should never be seen by someone who could be your potential employer, co-worker, or subordinate. That is not sexy!

ASSIGNMENT #20
YOUR CLOTHES

Buy one outfit that would be appropriate to wear to a job interview. If you need help picking out the right clothes, then ask someone at the store to help you. I have found from experience that many people who work at clothing stores really enjoy helping others look their best.

CHAPTER 21

YOUR INTERVIEWS

I'll never forget my first job interview. It was for a job at a department store. I wore some pants that were too tight, with some suspenders, a dress shirt, a tie, and some black dress shoes. The manager who interviewed me sat down across from me, and began to ask me some pretty straightforward questions.

She asked me, "so why should I hire you for this job?"

I answered, "Because I'm a prayer-warrior." Yes! I actually said that! That was pretty much the end of the interview. Needless to say, I didn't get the job.

I cringe whenever I think about that interview because it is so embarrassing. Why in the world did I think that being a "prayer-warrior" qualified me for a job selling clothes at a department store? Because no one ever told me how to prepare for an interview. I just didn't know what I would be asked.

In this chapter, I want to help you avoid making that kind of mistake in your interview. I want to share with you the only three questions that matter in an interview. There are three, and only three, questions that you will need to answer in an interview. They may be worded differently, but they come down to these following three questions:

1. Can you do the job?
2. Will you love the job?
3. Can I/we work with you?

The first question is about competence; the second is about commitment; and, the third is about chemistry. I'll say it again: every question that someone in an interview asks you can be boiled down to one of those three questions.

The first question is usually very indirect. The interviewer might say, "So, tell me about yourself." That is not the time to tell them that you love playing video games, unless you are interviewing for a job related to video games. That is not the time to tell them that you like long walks on the beach, and romantic candlelight dinners. What they want to know is, can you do the job, will you enjoy the job, and are you a team-player.

However you answer questions in an interview, make sure they are related to those three questions. Ask yourself, "which of the three questions are they asking me?"

If they ask you about your competence, tell them about any skills, abilities, education, or experiences you have that are related to the job for which you are interviewing.

Make sure you answer all your questions in a way that shows you are genuinely interested in the position. It wouldn't hurt to let them know how much you would enjoy doing that job. Let them know that your motive is not just to get a paycheck, but to learn and grow and help the company. People don't just want to hire someone who seems fickle. You want to let them know that you plan on sticking around, that you would genuinely enjoy working for their company.

You also want to make sure you carry yourself in manner that shows them you are easy to talk to, and easy to get along with. You might not have the right chemistry for that company. If you sense that you and the person with whom you are interviewing would not be a good fit, then don't try to fake it. Do your best to present your best self during the interview, but don't feel like you have to be phony. Be yourself, and hopefully you will be able to connect with the person who is interviewing you.

Make sure you are clear about the position for which you are interviewing. Learn as much as you can about the company. Do research about their mission, vision, and values. Learn about their services and their products. Learn about their history. Doing so will let the person with whom you are interviewing know that you have done your homework about the company. It will let them know that you have taken the initiative to learn about them. It will let them know that you are not just looking for a paycheck, but that you are genuinely interested in adding value to their company.

ASSIGNMENT #21
PREPARE FOR YOUR INTERVIEW

Think of a job you would like to have, then ask and answer the three questions: Can I do the job? Will I love the job? Is it easy to get along with me? Explain how your qualifications, your education, your background, your experiences, or your talents qualify you for the job. Explain how much you would enjoy doing that job.

CHAPTER 22
YOUR WEIGHTS

I used to run track. Before I began my workout, I used to train by tying a tire, and sometimes a parachute, around my waist, and running as fast as I could. The resistance from the tire or parachute made me a much stronger, faster runner. However, they also prevented me from running at my maximum potential. They slowed me down. When the time came for me to compete in various track meets, I not only took off my parachute and tire, I also took off anything that would slow me down. Why? Because I wanted to run as fast as I possibly could, and those weights would have slowed me down.

In the same way, you may have some things in your life that you need to take off because they are slowing you down, and preventing you from running at your maximum potential. Nothing is neutral except time. Either something is bringing you closer to realizing your dreams or it is pulling you further away from your dreams. It may not be a bad thing per se, but it is still weighing you down, or holding you back.

You may have some baggage that you need to put down. Perhaps you didn't pick it up on your own, maybe it was something that happened to you. Maybe you were abused as a child—told you were ugly, fat, or at least treated like you were, and it is hindering you, it's holding you back.

What is in your life that is weighing you down, or holding you back? What is in your life that needs to be cut off for your very survival? What is in your life—or who is in your life—that is holding you back? What is—or who is there—in your life that is about to lead you to destruction? What attitude, what mindset needs to be laid aside? What relationship needs to be cut off? What behavior needs to be eliminated? What habits need to be broken? What tendencies need to be tossed? What proclivities need to be pushed aside? What vocabulary words need to be removed?

To be sure, I am aware that you may have been hurt, and you have not been able to get over it. Perhaps you have been carrying the weight of that pain with you for a long time. The weight is very heavy, but because you have had it for so long, you have gotten used to carrying it. Maybe you have convinced yourself that you deserved it, that you are to blame for it, or something similar to that. I want to tell you that you are not to blame for many of the things that happened to you in your life.

I want you to be free—free from that misery, free from that depression, free from those feelings you have been carrying around. To do that, you have to make up your mind that you are so sick and tired of being sick and tired of that burden. You have to decide that you are going to do something to free yourself from it; that you are going to release it once and for all. You have to make up your mind that you are not going to let that burden or weight destroy you, and hold you back any longer.

ASSIGNMENT #22
YOUR WEIGHTS

If you need counseling, seek counseling. If you need to forgive someone, then begin working in that direction immediately. You must cut off, release, throw overboard, and destroy anything that is holding you back. If you don't release it, what are you going to miss out on? Take action today to begin addressing that burden.

When chasing your dreams, you have to press toward your goal. Pressing involves not merely unloading any unnecessary weight, but it also involves straining forward to attain your dreams. It involves perseverance, it involves heart, and it involves tenacity. It requires that you set your eyes on the goal that is in front of you, refusing to waver until you have reached that goal. The point that I want to make is that your goal must precede your pressing. That means that you must have your eyes on the goal before you begin pressing in that direction.

That might sound like common sense to you, but you would be surprised at how many people are busy but don't have any clear destination or goal in sight. They are just busy pressing without any clear direction. It is important to press toward your goal on a daily basis, or else someone else will have a goal for you to press toward. If you are not careful, you are going to burn out. There are so many things today that are being used to wear you out. There are people pulling you on your job; clubs asking you to do something; people pulling you to do this; other people pulling you to do that.

If you just pay attention to what you hear and see in the media for one day, you will see that music is telling us to do one thing, television another, and Internet still another. The tragedy is that we are getting pulled in so many directions that we end up burning ourselves out. We are so busy pressing in all kinds of different directions, that we don't realize that we are not pressing in the direction that matters.

In life, if you are not clear about your goal, then you will be running aimlessly, shadow-boxing a fake target that will wear you out.

I ask you, with love, what are you pressing toward? You ought not run aimlessly, or like someone boxing the air, without a clear target, or a clear goal. If you don't have the right goal in mind, then you are going to end up at the wrong destination. In what direction are you headed? Are you headed toward the goal of being what you were created to be?

ASSIGNMENT #23
YOUR PRESS

Make sure that you are pressing toward something that has real meaning and significance. While I have no problem with you getting rich or having nice things, I will have failed you if I did not tell you that you should live your life for something much bigger than money and things. I hope you are living your life to make this world a better place. I hope you are living your life to help other people. Please take some time today to reflect on your ultimate purpose in life. Are you living for things that have cosmic, or eternal significance? If not, then I want to encourage you to do some soul-searching today.

CHAPTER 24

YOUR STRUGGLE

A man found a cocoon of the emperor moth and took it home to watch it emerge. One day a small opening appeared, and for several hours the moth struggled but couldn't seem to force its body past a certain point.

Deciding something was wrong, the man took scissors and snipped the remaining bit of cocoon. The moth emerged easily, its body large and swollen, the wings small and shriveled. He expected that in a few hours the wings would spread out in their natural beauty, but they did not. Instead of developing into a creature free to fly, the moth spent its life dragging around a swollen body and shriveled wings.

The constricting cocoon and the struggle necessary to pass through the tiny opening are God's way of forcing fluid from the body into the wings. The "merciful" snip was, in reality, cruel. Sometimes the struggle is exactly what you need to prepare you for success. You don't get a degree without studying; you don't get a happy marriage without work; you don't get a happy home without sacrifice; you don't get in shape without exercise; you don't get good children without time; you don't teach good lessons without study; your promotion isn't going to come without hard work; your graduation isn't going to come without discipline. You have to go through something to get to your destination! Don't give up when the going gets tough; get tough and keep going!

The race to your dreams is not going to be easy. The word for race in Greek is where we get our word for "agony." Your race is going to be challenging. Sometimes you are going to cry, want to give up. However, when the going gets tough, remind yourself that the race to success is not a sprint; it is more like a marathon.

In high school, a friend of mine was selected to run the 800-meter race in a track meet against our cross-town rival. The problem was that he had never run the race before that day. The person who was supposed to run had injured himself and was unable to compete. So my willing and eager friend, positioned in the starting blocks, heard the gun, and burst out of the blocks like he had just stolen something. He sprinted, leaving all the other runners in the dust.

Literally, he was at least 100 meters ahead of everyone else on the track. Once he had run one lap (400 meters), he threw his hands in the air in total victory!

The problem was that he had another lap to go! We all began screaming at him, urging him to keep running. When it finally hit him that he needed to run another lap, he did his best to make it around the track one more time, but he was too tired to do so. All the other runners flew by him. It took him about four more minutes to make it to the finish line. While he was a fast runner, he failed to pace himself for the race that was at hand.

In your own journey to achieving your dreams, you need to pace yourself. You may want to put this book down today with great enthusiasm and begin "sprinting" toward your goal. You're saying in your head, "I'm going to lose 10 pounds this week; I'm going make one thousand dollars every day. The problem with trying to do too much too soon is that you will soon burn yourself out, and you will end up where you started off. Instead of sprinting, you need to pace yourself. Too many people are lying on the side of the road to their dreams because they started too fast.

You must condition yourself for the long haul, because the difference between successful people and unsuccessful people is the difference of their habits. Good habits are the secret of success. Therefore, form good ones, and become their slave. If you want to lose weight, start off realistically, and walk three days a week. After you have developed a good consistency, then try to pick up the length of the exercise, and the intensity. The habit—the consistency—will benefit you more in the long run than a spurt every now and then.

CHAPTER 26

YOUR FAILURES

Let's say you have tried something and you fail. What then? What do you do when something you have tried doesn't work? You first learn from the situation by figuring out how you got into the situation in the first place, and then ask yourself how you can avoid getting into that situation again. You need to learn to see your failures as education. Indeed, you need to learn how to fail forward by learning from your mistakes, getting up again, and trying something new. Don't allow yourself to get paralyzed by fear of failure. Rather, use fear as a means to motivate you to try something new.

Also, remember this: your failures will only hurt when you start blaming them on others. If you make a mistake, or if you blow it, take responsibility for it. It does no good for you to blame someone else for something that you did. Even if someone else helped you to fail, don't waste your time trying to point fingers. That will just waste your time, and probably create a whole lot of unnecessary drama in your life. The most successful people I know have no problem admitting they were wrong, and have no problem taking responsibility.

Learn to fail early and responsibly. That's what fear stands for: Failing Early And Responsibly. That means rather than missing out on the education that you could get from trying something new, take a risk, and if it doesn't work out, learn from it. That's what it means to fail responsibly. Learn from your mistakes, learn from what didn't work, and try something new. If that doesn't work, learn from it, and try something new.

Many great scientists failed thousands of times before they made a scientific discovery. You have to get comfortable with not getting it right the first time. Failure doesn't mean making a mistake; rather, failure is not getting up after you have made a mistake. That's massive failure. When you try something, and it doesn't work, turn the page, and write a new chapter in your life. Try something else. If that doesn't work, then try something else.

CHAPTER 27

YOUR GURKHA

To take action, you need to be courageous enough to take risks. In Nepal and India, there is a group of people known as Gurkhas. They are considered to be people who are naturally warlike and aggressive in battle, and possess resilience, physical strength, and courage, among other things.

In 1964, there was a war taking place between Malaysia and Indonesia. The Malaysian government asked a group of Gurkhas from Nepal if they would be willing to jump from transport airplanes into combat against the Indonesians. However, the Gurkhas had never been trained for that kind of combat. But the Gurkhas agreed to jump from planes under three conditions. "What are they?" asked the military officer. First, they said they would jump from the plane if it flew at a slow speed. Second, the land had to be marshy or reasonably soft and nowhere near rocky mountains because they were inexperienced at jumping from planes. The last thing the Gurkhas requested was that the planes fly only 100 feet from the ground.

The British soldier said that the Gurkhas would be dropped over a jungle, so their landing would be soft. Second, he said that the planes always fly as slowly as possible. Third, however, the British soldier said that it would not be wise for the planes to fly 100 feet from the ground because that would not give the parachutes enough time to open from that height.

The Gurkhas said, "Oh, that's all right then. With parachutes, we'll jump anywhere. Nobody said anything about parachutes before." The Gurkhas were willing to jump from planes without parachutes in order to win the war!

Everything worthwhile that I've ever done in life (everything!) ... initially scared me to death: speaking in public, going to college, getting jobs, getting married, having children. Don't let fear cripple you; press THROUGH your fears. There's SO MUCH more life and joy on the other side of your fears.

In this next chapter of your life, make sure you take courageous action. Be willing to try something to achieve your dreams that others would consider crazy. You need to be willing to take risks, and put yourself on the line. In the end, most people don't regret the things they did do; they regretted things they didn't do. They regretted the things they didn't try. Don't let that be you. Let the Gurkha in you come out.

CHAPTER 28

YOUR WORKS

There is a proverb that says, "Commit your works to the Lord, and your plans will succeed." The word "commit" literally means, "roll." In the Middle East, thousands of years ago, when someone died, and their body was laid to rest in a cave, people in those days would roll a big, heavy stone in front of the cave's entrance, to secure the body. They would "commit" that stone to the cave's entrance.

Sometimes our day-to-day duties seem so heavy, our responsibilities seem overwhelming, sometimes the little things you have to do every day seem so laborious and difficult that you don't have enough time in the day to get things done. You have to do your homework, memorize your playbook, go to that party, buy new clothes, pay your phone bill, exercise, cook, clean, wash, change the diaper, pay the bills, exercise, spend quality time, study, go to class, go to practice, find time to eat, pick the kids up, drop the kids off, pay the mortgage, grade papers, discipline kids, fix a sink, wash a car, an important appointment ... your weight just seems too heavy.

I want to encourage you to push our daily "works" to God. To roll our works to God means that you are doing it with God's will in mind. I believe that if we ask anything according to God's will, God will hears us and help us. If the boulders you are rolling are according to His will, He will establish your plans. He will bring them to pass, He will make them successful. If you are rolling your works to God, and your works are according to God's will, your plans will succeed.

There is no shortcut to your dreams. You need to plan your work; and work your plan. You are going to have to work hard every day to make it happen. Every day you wake up, you need to plan your day so that you can move one step closer to achieving an action strategy, an objective, a goal, and yes, your dreams. It will not be easy, but it is possible. The only place where "success" comes before "work" is in the dictionary.

Believe in yourself, take massive action, roll your plans to God, and sooner or later, you will find yourself enjoying the freedom and success you have always dreamed of.

Doing your best means giving your all, going all out, and not cutting corners. Doing your best means working as hard as you possibly can. If you work as hard as you possibly can, you will probably be working harder than others, because many people settle for doing "just enough." But don't be fooled—those who work the hardest often get more opportunities and freedom than those who do not, which usually results in more money and more success. Of course there was a time in America's history when this wasn't true. But today, it is truer than ever before.

Jerry Rice is the greatest wide receiver to ever play in the National Football League. He holds practically every record for his position. During his career, Rice broke so many records because he worked harder than most people in the off-season. When his opponents were traveling, resting, and enjoying the off-season, Jerry Rice worked out two times a day, six days a week. In the morning, he did a torturous five-mile trail-run, only stopping at the steepest section to do a series of ten forty-meter uphill sprints, before he completed the run. As the season approached, he stopped running the hill, and instead ran six one-hundred-yard sprints, six eighty-yarders, six sixtyyarders, six forty-yarders, six twenty-yarders, and sixteen ten-yarders with just two and a half minutes between sets. Then, he did three sets of ten repetitions of twenty different exercises—six days a week! To top it all off, he crawled across the parking lot to his car!

No matter how great you are, do your very best, and push yourself to the edges of your potential.

CHAPTER 30
YOUR HATERS

In life, you are going to have haters, but I want to give you a short word of advice about them. In life, there are going to be people who come into your life to do nothing more than discourage you. They are going to talk about you behind your back. They are going to try to hurt your feelings. They are going to lie about you. They are going to say mean, hateful things to you. They are going to try to get others to believe their lies. They are going to make fun of you, and mock you, and tease you, and even try to sabotage you. There are people in this world who, for whatever reason, are filled with jealousy, and envy, and hatred, and evil. My best advice to you is this: don't waste your time on them! Don't waste your breath arguing with someone like that. Don't waste your time trying to change their minds, because they are not interested in changing their minds; they are interested in disliking you. They are interested in making your life miserable.

I have had no shortage of hate-mail in my life from people who knew nothing about me. They were just jealous of my success, or resentful of it. Early in my work, I used to try to win them to my cause, but I have learned through the years that they were not interested in using reason. They were impervious when it came to calm, reasonable discussion. Their hatred and selfishness blinded them from logical dialogue. They constantly made personal attacks about me and my family.

Consequently, after I tried reasoning with them to no avail, I often found myself too tired to complete the work that really mattered. My best advice to you whenever you encounter a hater, is to focus on what you believe you are called to do. Focus on your dreams. Focus on your goals. Focus on your beliefs. Focus on your family. Focus on your loved ones. Focus on those people you are really trying to serve.

Now, having said that, let me say something else about haters. Not everyone who disagrees with you is hating on you. No, some people who disagree with you really do love you, and really do have your best interest at heart. They really do want you to succeed. When someone you love, and who loves you, disagrees with you in a loving way, don't dismiss them as "haters." Doing so will only set you up for some problems later. Labeling all those who disagree with you as haters can set you up for failure.

The question becomes, how can you tell the difference between a hater and someone who has your back? There are no easy answers to that, but I think one way is to ask yourself, "does this person have a history of believing in me and having my back?" If the answer is yes, then I want to encourage you to take what they say to you very seriously. Don't just dismiss them. Don't disregard their opinion, because they might see something, or say something, that could really position you to succeed.

In any case, try to maintain a balance between confidence and humility. Be confident enough to chase your dreams, but humble enough to receive honest feedback from those you love. Their advice could help you grow as a person, could help you save a lot of money, or make a lot of money. Their input could help you discover an approach that makes you more effective and efficient.

Let me say one more thing about haters. Some haters might say something that is true about you. As angry or hurt as you might be by their words, I want to encourage you to go to a private, quiet place and reflect soberly about whether anything your "haters" are saying is true. If any of their criticisms are true, then please humble yourself, and admit that they are right. Now, you don't have to let them know you have seen the error of your ways; you just need to make sure you are correcting yourself, so that you can become the best you that you can be.

Finally, don't despise your haters. They can become your elevators. They can become your escalators. They can help you become better, stronger, and wiser, on your way to your dreams. See all criticisms as an opportunity for you to learn and grow.

I have grown more from my failures and my critics than from anything else. There is something about their hatred and bitterness that has motivated me to prove them wrong. They have often inspired me to focus even more. They have often helped me improve as a person. They've help me become more patient, more driven, more forgiving, and more gracious.

At this stage in my life, I have had several haters come into my life. Some of them are in my family. Some of them have been classmates. Some of them have been colleagues. Some of them have been friends. All of them have helped me grow.

They have been like my sandpaper people. Sandpaper people are those people who rub you the wrong way, who get on your last nerve. Avoiding them is impossible sometimes, so all you can do is trust they are in your life for a reason; and, perhaps that reason is to help you grow into the person you were meant to be.

Maybe one day, you will be able to thank them for hating on you. Maybe one day you will be able to come back, and thank them. Thank them for putting you down, because their hatred motivated you to rise up and work harder. Their resentment inspired you to prove them wrong. Their negativity prompted you to achieve greatness. Don't despise your haters; just don't waste too much time responding to them.

Instead, focus on your dreams, your goals, your priorities. If you are going to spend any time thinking about them, then let it be in ways that can help you grow. I've learned that it's hard to hate someone that you are praying for. I've prayed for a lot of my haters, that they would one day find peace in their hearts and joy in their lives. Hurt people, hurt people, and many haters are just hurting people. Engaging them often is a waste of time; but praying for them is not.

One of my favorite poems says:

The test of a man is the fight that he makes,
The grit that he daily shows.
The way he stands upon his feet,
And takes life's numerous bumps and blows.
A coward can smile when there's nought to fear,
For nothing his progress bars;

But it takes a man to stand and cheer,
While the other fellow stars.
It isn't the victory after all,
But the fight that a brother makes;
A man when driven against the wall,
Still stands erect and takes
The blows of fate, with his head held high,
Bleeding and bruised and pale;
Is the man who will win, fate defied,
For he isn't afraid to fail.

My friend, don't worry about haters. I have intentionally put them near the end this book because they don't deserve any priority in your life. Instead, I want you to focus. Focus on your dreams. Focus on your family. Focus on your faith. Focus! Focus on where you are going. Your time will be much better spent.

CHAPTER 31
YOUR NEXT CHAPTER

In this book, I have tried to share with you my understanding of how to turn the page and write a new chapter in your life. I have shared with you tools and techniques that I have used to turn my own life around, and tools I have seen others use to turn their lives around too. I have shared with you the things I believe you need to be, things you need to know, and things you need to do in order to create the life of your dreams. I have tried to show you what you will need in order to create a new chapter in your life that is filled with perseverance and possibility, with success and significance.

I started off by sharing my own story with you, and telling you how I turned the page, and began a new chapter in my own life. I then asked you to get clear about your own story; and, I called you to turn the page. I called you to commit to proactively creating the life of your dreams, and to cut yourself off from any other possibilities. I called you to take responsibility for your life.

I then laid the foundation of upon which I believe you should build your life: faith, love, gratitude, humility, integrity, honesty, self-discipline.

Next I asked you to identify your dreams, and told you about your need to believe in yourself. I encouraged you to eliminate your limiting beliefs, and to keep a positive mental attitude. I also encouraged you to be vigilant about the environment that you allow yourself to be exposed to, because it can affect greatly, good and bad.

Then I helped you put together a roadmap to your success. A roadmap to get you from here to there.

Then I encouraged you to educate yourself by learning about what you need to learn in order to become who you need to become, so that you can do what you need to do. I encouraged you to be careful about your friendships, and to make sure you find mentors who have already done what you would like to do.

Then I called you to take action. I called you to do something about your plan. I called you to not only plan your work, but also to work that plan. I called you to take massive action, to pour your heart, your soul, your mind, and your strength into making your next chapter one filled with everything you dreamed of.

I talked about your appearance, your interviews, your weights, your press, your struggles, your pace, your failures, your gurkha, your works, being your best, and then we talked about your haters.

ASSIGNMENT #24
YOUR TURN!

Now it's on you, my friend. It's on you to take all that I've shared with you, and to put it to good use. It's time for you to close this book, and get to work. It's time for you to stop dwelling on your past and start working toward your future. It's time for you to get up and take life by the hand and dance. It's time for you to get in your plane and fly. It's time for you to spread your wings and rise above the clouds.

I can't live your life for you. Now is your time. This is your moment. This is the moment that will separate you from everyone else.

So, turn the page. Write now. Action may not always bring happiness, but there is no happiness without action. Stop TALKING about what you're "gonna" do, "finna" do and "need" to do. DO IT! The secret of getting ahead ... is simply getting started. So get started. Turn the page! Write Now!

AFTERWORD

I have no doubt you will go far if you apply the things I've written about in this book. I haven't done so bad myself. For that I am very grateful.

There's an old song that I love so much. It says,

> If I can help somebody as I pass along,
> If I can cheer somebody with a word or song,
> If I can show somebody he is trav'ling wrong,
> Then my living shall not be in vain.

These words are precious to me because they remind me that true success and significance will not be measured by material things, but, in the final analysis, success will be measured by how much we have given our lives in service to others.

In this book, I have tried to help you on your journey to significance and success; I have tried to point out things that may be blocking you from reaching your dreams; and, I have tried to cheer you with words that are life-giving and transformational. If I have done even one of these things for you, then for that I'm grateful; and, my living has not been in vain.

I'd love to hear how this book has helped you. If you have a story that illustrates a point I've made in this book, I'd love to read it. Feel free to send me your thoughts or stories at: ync@mannyscott.com.

ABOUT THE AUTHOR

An original Freedom Writer whose story is told in part in the 2007 hit movie, *Freedom Writers*, Manny Scott has energized over a million leaders, educators, volunteers, and students worldwide with his authentic, inspiring messages of hope. As the founder and CEO of Ink International, Manny Scott has spoken for the past fifteen years to hundreds of groups a year. He is the speaker of choice for conferences, conventions, schools, fundraisers, and banquets.

He is happily married to Alice, and they have three children. He is a successful entrepreneur, a pilot, a Ph.D. student, and one of the nation's most sought after speakers.

For more info and resources to help you
turn the page, contact us at:
Ink International
P.O. Box 464868
Lawrenceville, GA 30042
Phone: (888) 987-TURN
Or visit our website at:
www.MannyScott.com

37594936R00124

Made in the USA
San Bernardino, CA
21 August 2016